———— PUBLIC LIBRARY ————

Presented to the
Library
by

PubWest

Analekta
an anthology of writing

Molalla, Oregon

Analekta—Volume 4

Copyright © 2015

All rights to this anthology are reserved. No part of this book may be reproduced in any form or by any electronic or mechanical means, including information storage and retrieval systems, without written permission from the authors or publisher.

Rights to the individual works contained in this anthology are owned by the submitting authors and each has permitted the work's use in this collection.

ISBN: 978-0-9907073-6-3

eISBN: 978-0-9907073-7-0

Printed in the United States of America Boho Books edition/ November 2015

Contents

Introduction vii

Fiction
Glen L. Bledsoe
    Scoop de Ville 6
Rebekkah Brainerd
    Earth Sea Sky 14
Erin Devlin
    Secrets I Couldn't Keep 22
Lynn Blatter
    A La Carte 39
Kate Gray
    Don't Mistake Tenderness For Weakness 42
Devon Seale
    Morning Ritual 60
Kelly Samarah
    Hailey 63
Dani Clifton
    Deadly Deals 85

Fiction Novel Excerpts
John Flavin
    The Big World 53
Jacqueline Carl
    Seasons Of The Wild 75
Esther Wood
    Useful Equipment 78

Nonfiction
Angie Hughes
    The Right To Mourn 1
Heather L. Nelson
    Lost Family: Found! 29

Poetry

John Sibley Williams
    Calligraphy 4
    In Apology 5
    Things Start At Their Names 28
    Salmon Run 62

Rick Carl
    The Reaper 11
    Eagles 59
    Crows 77

Larry Anderson
    Rose Garden In The Foothills 13
    Cold Night, Little Owl 41

Nichelle Halseth
    Shared Perspective 18
    Intermission 20
    An Invitation 57
    Her, Not Her 73

Susan Sweetland Garay
    An Ordinary Thing 38

Sandra Rokoff-Lizut
    Definitions 52
    When Will Your *Real* Life Begin 84

Contributors 95
Our Thanks 101
Submission Guidelines 103

Introduction

Once again, writers along the highways and byways of Oregon have filled *Analekta*-Volume 4's pages with a rich mix of words; a harvest of story, poetry, and nonfiction as diverse as the state in which it grew. Featuring both new and returning contributors, this volume represents a wide-ranging view into the human experience.

Our Featured Author is Kate Gray, author of the highly acclaimed *Carry the Sky*, a novel that sings a brave and honest anthem about what it means to be different in a world of uniformity. Her first full-length book of poems, *Another Sunset We Survive* (2007), was a finalist for the Oregon Book Award and followed chapbooks *Bone-Knowing* (2006), winner of the Gertrude Press Poetry Prize, and *Where She Goes* (2000), winner of the Blue Light Chapbook Prize. Her poetry and essays have also been nominated for the Pushcart Prize. In addition to her own writing, Kate generously shares her skills and nurturance of other writers through workshops and consultation.

We are thrilled to feature such a talented author and hope that all budding authors out there are inspired by what she has wrought.

Happy reading!

~L. Lee Shaw & Heather Frazier, *Analekta* Editors

The Right To Mourn
Angie Hughes

MY SISTER, ALLISON, AND I wipe the pink flesh of the new baby and Allison just keeps saying over and over, "What the fuck, Angie? What the fuck?" Tears are on our cheeks and the baby is crying—maybe from the shock of the wet wipe on her sweet little bottom, or maybe from the chaos she feels all around her. She is only five days old and her older sister has just died in a room down the hall.

They call it tracheal stenosis, and the type Sara has is very rare. Yet, at one, she is diagnosed on a Monday and dies on a Thursday. Her baby sister, born this very week, will never know what it's like to have a big sister, but she will undoubtedly suffer from the stories, the loss, and the missing piece that exists almost entirely before she does.

My cousin and her little family gather earlier in the week, babies touching cheek to cheek, for the first and last time, as breath is running out for big sister Sara. The children's garden at the hospital is a peaceful place—a nice setting for those last family photos. We all watch from the windows for a while, until it is decided that she is going to breathe on for a little longer, and we are allowed in to see her. Perhaps forty people gather around, some singing, some crying, some too buried in their grief to give anything.

We all love this little girl, but we are not mom, dad, or even grandma. We are the cousins, the friends, the great-aunts. Who are we to grieve? We all try to establish our place in the pecking order of mourning. We start to cry, we start to break down, but then we check ourselves, asking if we really have the right. Our self-deprecation plays out in these waiting rooms, behind glass walls, trying to figure out who knows them best, who loves Sara the most, and at some point, I just can't take it. We should all grieve in our own way—differently but equally loving and mourning the loss of this beautiful little girl, as she lies dying down the hall. Some don't think so, as arguments break out, dramas ensue, and camps are established over five days down sterile halls.

Allison and I try to find quiet places to hold vigil when we can, in rooms separate from the rest of the group. Maybe we are the ones with the problem and we lay claim to our grief more than we should. The truth is, no one knows how to behave right now, and this is *the* unimaginable hell we all refer to when we look at our own babies and feel relief that "it's not happening to us."

On the final night with Sara, her mama won't leave her side as she breathes out the last of her strangled little life. In the waiting room, we face a situation. The new baby is hungry—so hungry her blood curdling screeches become overwhelming. My sister looks at me. I know what she is thinking. She hesitantly asks, "Should I?" Those gathered around begin to pay attention and everyone offers their idiosyncratic opinions about the prospect of my sister breastfeeding this new baby. Luckily, Allison still has a supply of milk from feeding her own healthy one-year-old. Those in the room are in agreement that she should, and the support is overwhelming as we all cry. We begin to mourn together. Somehow, the idea of my sister breastfeeding this new baby, not her own, breaks through all the personality barriers we've been experiencing and we become a village behind the glass wall.

Allison feeds the baby, who latches on right away and stays content for hours after. The amount of support and encouragement for my sister, from everyone in the room, is emotionally saturating. Mama hears word of this from Sara's room and is overcome with grateful thanks. She just wants to spend these last moments with her girl, with no distractions, and my sister is able to make this possible. She knows that her new baby is taken care of, so, exhausted, spent, and overwhelmed, she can focus on the last of her life with her little angel. One simple, final sigh, and it is reported, through howls of anguish, that she is gone.

We find ourselves diapering the new baby, who is precariously balanced on a counter in the bathroom, and Allison becomes lost in her own grief again. She just keeps saying, "What the fuck?" completely dazed, because none of it feels real. We separate and find lonely corners, returning to our singular grief.

The memory of that week—the birth, the death, and the sight of my sister breastfeeding a baby with tears rolling down her cheeks—has changed everything for me. I see Allison differently; though she is my little sister, she grew up, completely, in that moment. I have never felt more respect for a human being than I felt for her right then, and I don't think I could ever take her for granted again. She bonded a group, she fed a child, and she relieved a mother in her deepest grief. I feel I was only observing this beautiful picture, an assistant to my sister's monumental gift, but I was part of something that will always change my thinking from what it might have been. I live a little more every day because of Sara. I give a little more because of my sister. I know that if we are all living, then we have so much less to complain about. I continue to mourn, and I believe I always will—and I have the right to mourn—but our shared grief, in rare moments when we all gather and talk, brings me back to that deep feeling of beauty, appreciation, and profound respect for what we all experienced together.

Calligraphy
John Sibley Williams

All these elegant black
forms / isolated universes
beholden to every other /
each twisted oak limb that haunts
night's grass and is part
of a body / the unfinished
chrysalis of river water becoming
sea / I cannot follow my
line's trail into meaning without
injury / to write you into the world
would imply continuity / and I'm not ready
to reconcile fatherhood with the hope
of a son / ink spills into the next / shadows
stand guard at the root of each object
and the light

In Apology
John Sibley Williams

Some fears cannot be conveyed without metaphor—
                so please accept these

golden threads woven into a bundle, hundreds
of thousands of compact threads that compose
a single bale. Each holds tight its brilliance, initiates
yet succumbs in the end to the brilliance
of the whole. Body upon brilliant body. Bone sparked
against bone, a quiet fire over a field
        so flat and forever.

*

Not even earth can describe our harvest, not even the sky
in all its burning can speak for ash.
              But there comes a time
abstractions must choose what shape to take.

For *justice*, please look down into my hands
as into a mirror. For *truth*, here's
a cord of kindling. For *you*, a midnight river of stars.
Impermanent knowledge brilliant disrepair fire—

I am sorry I am sorry I am

so sorry for describing *us* as bundled and aflame
and the beginning and end of light. *Light* is flat and forever
as a tree's shadow at sunset.

Scoop de Ville
Glen L. Bledsoe

I AM A SOLDIER IN the *Army of Gaia*. Although our numbers are small, we do good work. We don't, however, always follow the Letter of the Law.

I burn cars—not for recreation, although it may give me a kind of pleasure. Not just any car, but only those vehicles considered by the AoG to be AANs—*Abominations Against Nature*. Gas guzzlers. Animated man-toys of steel, plastic, rubber and jacked attitude. Testosterone-mobiles. The Hummer is only the most blatant example of entitled America not playing well with Mother Earth, but there are others. Too many others.

They picked me up in a battered 1992 Geo Metro in front of Reed Opera House in Salem. I gave Carson as my name although it was not my real name, which they were well aware. Neither was Steve the name of the thin man with the cut of an aging cowboy. Nor was Kim, our driver, the name of the large, bland, shapeless person who might have been either a man or a woman (it was impossible to tell which). Steve looked like he was from up the Gorge. Kim was probably from Portland or more likely Seattle. These could very well be disguises, too. We'd never met before, nor would we ever meet again, in all likelihood.

We headed south on I-5, Steve searching for rockabilly on the radio. No one spoke much along the long, empty stretch between Albany and Eugene, which was probably just as well. The less we knew about each other, the less there was to tell should we be caught. That's the way the AoG always worked it. Cells.

Eugene was our destination. According to our sources, three AANs (all Hummers) one white, one black, and one cherry red—were located in a used car lot on Empire Park Drive. If all went well, we would send a blazing signal to America that the time was now to renounce our wasting ways.

As we approached the Coburg exit, Steve said, "Let's stop at Scoop de Ville."

Kim shot him a puzzled look.

"Scoop de Ville makes the best milk shakes in the state. I always stop and get one when I go to Eugene. And you can get *pumpkin* flavor this time of year."

"There's no time," Kim said in a high-pitched voice, with a dismissive wave of the hand.

"We *make* time for quality ice cream," Steve said with authority and nodded at the exit sign. "It's not far off the road. It'll just take five minutes. Besides, I haven't eaten since breakfast."

"Okay by me," I said from the backseat. My bladder suggested that we make a stop for additional reasons as well.

Kim shrugged and steered onto the exit ramp. "If it takes a second over five minutes, I leave you, and you hitchhike back."

"I'll pick you up a Chocky-Cream Bar. What do you say?" Steve said and winked. "I bet you'd like that."

"Pineapple shake," Kim said. "With a straw *and* a spoon."

Steve nodded after a moment's thought. "All right. I pick up my Social Security check Thursday so I can afford to be generous tonight. It's on me."

We drove just under the 45 mph speed limit delineated by a traffic sign pockmarked with bullet holes. A white pickup flying an oversized American flag passed us as if we were standing still. Kim pulled into the parking lot where a pink neon sign in the shape of an ice cream cone flickered unappetizingly. A cartoon mural on the side of a squat block building showed a banana-yellow, mid-50s Coupe de Ville Cadillac with an oversized ice cream cone projecting from its roof.

Kim killed the engine.

"I'll just be a minute," Steve said as he opened the door and spryly ducked out of the car.

"Pit stop," I said, and opened my door. I stood and scanned the side of the building for a sign that said MEN. Finding none, I walked around the front to the other side.

A man and woman in their twenties stood face-to-face. He was red-haired, tall, and slim with a scraggly wisp of a beard on his chin. She was seven or eight months pregnant.

"You're coming with me, you little shit," Red said, and shoved the woman against the wall.

She wrapped her arms protectively around her belly. Her dark eyes went wide under a tangle of dishwater-blond hair. She never made a sound. She'd been through this before.

Something clicked in my head. I tapped him on the shoulder and said, "Excuse me, but I'm going to have to ask you to keep your hands to yourself."

He didn't bother to turn his head in my direction, but glared at the young woman. He said over his shoulder, "You don't understand. I have to bring her back. I *have* to. She's been bad. She tried to run away again." To punctuate his statement, he slammed her against the wall.

"I don't have to understand. I can see with my own eyes what you're doing. Talk to her all you want, but *keep your hands off the lady*."

He faced me with his hands on his hips. "All you tree hugging hippies want to do is tell everyone else what to do. Mind your own goddam business."

I folded my arms. Of course, if this broke into a fight, I could be jeopardizing the mission. Fuck the mission.

Out of the corner of my eye, I saw Kim pull the Geo Metro into a nearby parking slot.

"I'm sick to death of people like you telling me what to do," said Red and struck an ornate fighting pose. "I have to warn you, I have a black belt."

"I wipe my arse with black belts every day," I said evenly, and assumed a boxer's stance. It was a bit of hyperbole, of course. More like five out of seven days. I like my weekends free.

"Oh, Mr. George Foreman!" Red said sarcastically, but I'd shaken him with my comment.

The young lady took the opportunity to slip away and that really should have been enough for me. If Red had turned and walked away, I suppose I would have let him go.

But I didn't *want* him to go. Something powerful inside me wanted to hurt him, hurt him and every other man who brutalized and battered women all over the world. I'm all about justice, if you hadn't guessed by now.

Kim stepped out of the car, guided the woman into the passenger's seat and quietly drove away. I never saw either of them again. She's doubtless been given a new name, a new life in a community far away from here. That's another thing AoG does. We don't just burn cars.

Steve sauntered around the corner with two white paper cups in his hands. He sized up the situation, leaned against a parked car, and casually sipped at one with a faint smile on his face.

"I warned you," Red said, and kicked at me. It was slow and weak. Apparently he had taken a few kick-tag karate classes. Maybe he was even a black belt. They just about give them away these days. I flicked his foot away with my forearm, stepped forward and with a twist of my waist, bounced my weight through my right arm. My fist connected with his jaw. I felt it flex under my knuckles and the shock shivered through his body. I expected him to drop, but instead he snapped forward and shoved me. Surprised, I took a step back, tripped over something, and rolled onto my back. He leaped on me and tried to hold my hands down like a schoolyard bully, but he had no strength after the tap on the jaw. As long as he held my wrists he couldn't use his hands to pull a knife, if he had one. My hands, feebly held, were for all intents and purposes free.

With little effort, I forced my thumbs into the corners of his mouth and used my nails to begin to peel back his gums. He had no leverage to pull my hands away and so tried to retreat by standing up. That was fine with me, only I wasn't going to lie on the ground while he stood and kicked me. I grabbed his shirtfront for the ride, and it ripped as he rose and pulled me to my feet.

He kept his distance and continued to flick roundhouse kicks, which bounced harmlessly off my arms. I closed the gap, striking him at will, humiliating him at every opportunity. Slapping him open-handed. Flipping him under the nose. Poking him in his chest with my index finger. I wanted him to feel what it was like to be pushed around.

At last, shirt shredded, jaw swollen, with blood trickling from the corners of his mouth, he broke into tears. He shook his fist at me. "I'm going to get you!" They all say that. Every bully that ever got a comeuppance repeats that empty threat. He feigned a lunge toward me, then dodged for the car that Steve leaned against.

"You're a witness," Red said to Steve and jumped into the driver's seat. "He attacked me. I'm calling the police."

Steve said, "I'd call the police if I were you. Yes, sir. I would."

But Red wouldn't call the police. He knew I'd tell them what he'd been doing, and he might be headed for a little jail time—especially if he were a repeat offender, which was likely.

The engine spluttered to life, and the Ford Galaxie with mismatched door panels chugged out of the parking lot without stopping onto the roadway, only to be struck broadside by a white pickup truck going considerably faster than the posted speed limit. Probably the same vehicle that passed us when we first arrived. Auto parts old and new skittered over the blacktop. The American flag that had streamed so valiantly behind now hung torn over one side of the windshield like a pirate's eye patch. Doors popped open in both vehicles and their respective drivers rose angrily to their feet. Red beat his fists in fury on the hood of the pickup truck until the driver reached toward his rifle rack.

Sirens whined in the near distance.

Red would get his chance to speak to the police, although I would bet money the topic *uninsured motorist* would be the centerpiece of the dialog.

Steve handed me a cup. "I hope you like pineapple," he said, listening to the men vilify each other's ancestors.

He pulled out a cell phone and said, "I'll put a call in and get somebody to pick us up. The Hummers'll have to wait till another day. It's been a good night's work, though, even so. Too bad *those* weren't Hummers, but a pickup truck and a junker are atrocities and will do just as well. Especially the white pickup. People driving white pickup trucks flying the stars and stripes out their ass-ends do have some *attitude*."

It hadn't been a good night's work though. Not really. Red would find another woman to abuse some other time and some other place. He would vent his anger at what happened this night on her again and again. I served no purpose other than to add fuel to the fire.

Yet it was something that needed doing so I did it, and I would do it again if the situation repeated. I had Red's license plates memorized. I'd look him up later using AoG resources, find out his name, where he lived, and in a month or so I'd pay him a visit to see just how he was behaving himself.

The Reaper
Rick Carl

Some call him the Angel of Death
Others say the Grim Reaper
Whatever you call him it's my job to see
That he doesn't make you a keeper

We've all heard the stories
Of when life finally hits the wall
But what you heard ain't the way it is
When the reaper comes to call

I've stared death square in the face
It's like the cold winds of the fall
And the darkness overcomes us
When the reaper comes to call

It's been many a time I've seen the signs
When death is a ringing its pall
As one of my men tries to console
You know you can't save them all

We take an oath to do no harm
And when summoned answer the call
Yet still we try and try again
And lose when we've given our all

The odds are in his favor
The chances of winning small
But you do your best to save a life
When the reaper comes to call

Some might call him an angel
Some say that he is not
But when you've looked into his eyes
You realize what life's all about

It saddens and sickens every twist of fate
Every loss hurts a little bit more
When we get there just a little too late
It strikes all the way to our core

But wait there's a light at the end of this road
We've truly done a lot of good
There are people walking this earth today
That without us never would

They say that when your number is up
There's nothing that you can do
But I've spent a good part of my life
Making sure he misses his cue

The moral is there are people out there
Fighting hard to deny him his due
And are always willing to risk their life
To make sure he doesn't get to you

Rose Garden In The Foothills
Larry Anderson

A sultry evening in the foothills,
we park along Red Rock Road.

Up the road, a porch light flickers,
dogs bark, motorcyclists
race to fading red-orange sunset.

We sneak under a barbed wire fence,
avoid lurking nettles, poison ivy,
drop to our rose garden, settle.

As lipstick, roses, Chianti Classico
abandon singular color to night,

disparate fragrances
yield to strange attractors
in vestiges of a crimson sun.

Earth Sea Sky
Rebekkah Brainerd

MY HEAD BROKE THE SURFACE of the water. I tried to cough once and my body seized, water forcing itself out of any place it could escape. Panicked pressure forced liquid to vomit out of my mouth and nose while I gasped and desperately clawed for air. This had to be saltwater. It *burned*.

My mind raced. Trying to remember. To remember *anything* of what was going on.

"There, there. Just breathe." Said a male voice, and with a convulsive shock I realized I was clinging to a hard, warm body.

People. People on the beach when I wasn't supposed to be near the ocean. Male people on the beach that looked at me with silvery marks painted on their bodies.

Water Men.

Abruptly, I was moved; hands passing me, or maybe hands grabbing me. I shrieked, a painfully small sound, expelling what precious air I had managed to regain. I was jerked out of the water and onto a hard surface, hands letting me go. I gasped and choked on the hard ground, shaking and shuddering, trying to stop the noises I was making. For several moments I couldn't make my mind think, could only relish in the sweet blessedness of air.

But I needed to open my eyes. Needed to figure out what the hell was *going on.*

Open eyes!

My eyelids felt swollen, and prying them open was difficult. I was lying on a dark green platform that looked like a giant lily pad. The whole small room looked to be made of giant lily pads, with half of the floor cut away to reveal the dark salt water. I wasn't sure where the light was coming from.

Sitting on the edge was a man with blue-green fins coming off of his head and running down his back and arms, a blue and green tail for a lower body. I felt my eyes go wide and made a small sound I tried not to let out.

"Is she of Earth?" Another male voice asked behind me and I convulsed again: *Not more!* I tried to move, managed to shift my weight onto my hands. I could hear the sounds of other bodies getting out of the water.

My kidnapper scoffed. "Of course she's of Earth. I wouldn't have brought her otherwise."

"I'm sure you haven't forgotten that Earth-Sky crosses can sometimes have no wings." The first speaker said in an irritated voice. There was a pause, and he said more quietly: "It's hard to tell, she's so slight."

"She's Earth People, I saw her village." My kidnapper pulled his long tail out of the water and up onto the same platform I was lying on, leaning back on his hands. "I found her wandering the beaches alone."

The beaches. The beaches that my mother always told me to stay away from because Water People would kidnap Earth People to be taken away as…

In a jerky movement, I was on my hands and knees, the world tilting wildly in my attempt, trying desperately to angle myself back into the water. I had to get out of here; I had to get back to—

An arm wrapped around my waist and yanked me back. "Not so fast, little one," said another voice kindly. *Not another!* "You won't survive on your own out there by yourself."

Turning my head towards my second captor, I was aware of yellow and orange striped fins and tail, and vivid green eyes. Then I noticed another figure behind him, leaning against the wall next to a hallway that led from here. A jolt of hope soared through me: he had legs. He was Earth People. He had to be! I locked eyes with the blonde and blue-eyed man.

"Help," I rasped, my throat was still on fire from the salt water. He frowned slightly and I struggled against the hands holding me, not understanding why he wouldn't *help* me. I had to get out of this place, he had to be Earth people—

There was a laugh. "Is she seriously asking *you* for help?"

That's when I saw my kidnapper's change. He no longer had fins on his arms or head; in its place was pink skin and light brown hair. His tail was melting away, the flesh paling and the scales dissipating into skin, separating into two equal parts. Toes, knees, and hips solidified and the familiar shape of leg muscles formed out of disappearing tissue. Then my kidnapper got to his *feet* and I couldn't force myself to look away from his nakedness as my mind refused to believe it.

Two more men were now getting to their feet out of the water, color of orange and green fading on the new skin of their legs. My head whipped around to stare at the man currently holding me tightly by the shoulders. My headed pounded sickly at the sudden movement. The orange and yellow was disappearing and fading on him, too.

My eyes jumped to the blonde man by the door. I was such a fool; I had never seen an Earth with blonde hair or blue eyes, and he had silvery marks across his shoulders, neck, and up onto his jaw. He wasn't Earth People at all. I was trapped.

My mother had told me of this. Even Ava had told me never to wander the beaches alone! Ava, with her beautiful golden curls and pure white wings, who grinned at me wickedly and told me that she'd marry me off to her brother so we would be sisters for real...

Swallowing hard, my vision began to blur. How could I have been so stupid? Lulled by the sound of the ocean day after day, I had ignored the warnings of my village, and now I was paying the price.

The blonde Water Man was frowning at me and I hurriedly blinked away the wetness. I would not be weak and show tears.

"Where am I?" I swallowed against the burn of my throat.

Out of the corner of my eye, I saw my original captor look up, but it was the blonde who spoke: "You are in the city of Alexandria, deep under the ocean."

Getting enough air was difficult. "*Why?*"

I waited for him to confirm what I already knew.

"I'll take her to the other women," My kidnapper said. "They can help calm her down and start the transition."

The blonde was still holding eye contact. I broke it as the Water Man holding me let go and I saw him get to his feet. I pulled myself away from him, putting my legs under me. I needed to get back into the water and get away from this place.

A hand was suddenly offered, palm up in front of me. It was so similar to the gentlemanly gesture from home that I placed my own palm in his automatically. The blonde Water Man pulled me to my feet, and I had to lock my knees to keep myself from falling over. He slowly released my hand. I avoided eye contact and glanced at the water a couple feet from where I stood, my heart pounding like a tiny bird trapped in my chest.

"I take it none of the rest of you were successful?" The blonde asked the other Water Men.

"I had one," Another Water Man muttered, "A Sky People scout destroyed the transport and I lost her. Nicked the other transport and it didn't make it all the way down. That's why she"—I saw him jerk his chin at me—"looks half-drowned."

My heart leapt. Ava had to be looking for me if a scout from the Sky People knew someone had been taken! If I could make it out of here, Ava would be able to find me.

"Tomorrow, I expect the rest of you—"

I hit the water so hard it hurt. For a second, I didn't sink, wincing in pain, and I frantically tried to orient myself. I furiously kicked my feet to get myself under water, and lunged deeper. The water was horrible, freezing cold and hurting against my skin, making me start to panic for air. My eyes burned in the salt, but I fought against the urge to close them.

The wall of the room arched below the surface of the water, but ended a few feet down. There was the edge! I beat my legs furiously, grabbed the edge of the wall, and hauled myself underneath into the bigger water and freedom.

All around me were structures made of the same giant lily pads. Light gleamed through clear windows, the structures connected by hallways made of glass or some material I had never seen before. People moved in and between, sometimes together, sometimes alone. Water People and fish of every color, shape, and size darted through the water outside these rooms. And beyond these interconnected structures resembling an elaborate display of a spider's web, was blackness. Never ending blackness of water, in every direction I could see. No sunlight penetrated the dark depths to guide me back home.

Something seized me. I shrieked, bubbles exploding from my mouth in a flurry of crystal spheres of distorted sound. I fought against the force that drug me backwards up into the little room with the floor cut away, but the grip did not relent.

My head broke the surface of the water.

Shared Perspective
Nichelle Halseth

I hear you calling in the silence like an aftertaste of our conversations
that I don't want to rinse out of my mouth
Gargle—Rinse—Repeat
It feels complete when you pick up what I put down moments ago
But
I always feel the need to restate,
Solitude can happen even in a crowded room full of strangers… or
friends
So when you receive these messages do me a favor
Breathe
Every time you think of me, breathe
and remember that you don't need your hands to fly
only your wings

The moon is closing in on this soft-lit space and casts shadows of our
bodies on a blank canvas
They dance
They dance across bedsheets and textured walls catching their reflection in windows thirty-seven stories above ground, laughing
                        Laughing
Laughing how they used to laugh when the world didn't seem so small
Before the best pieces of themselves were kept in Mason jars with
colorful ribbons labeled numerically along with a note attached that says,
                "For Emergency Use Only"
We used a vault to hide our past, scared to go inside and lose ourselves
in the picture frames of fate, no strength to clean up circumstance,
imagining only the faces we saw on each other the moment we took
our masks off
                The Sweetest Dream!
You tasted every word that came from my mouth and I found color
in your touch stretching in every direction to misrepresent the wild
images of our present Self projecting things that haven't occurred yet
This feeling of control has become instinctual so let us save the
imperfections

Call it you
Call it unfinished
Call it blame
I will gladly take it

Intermission
Nichelle Halseth

My heart cracked a little
Caught itself bleeding all over my other organs
finger painting your name in Sanskrit
It meant to say, "You can't leave"
but you heard me say "You are a leaf"
So with the next breeze, I took you into my bedroom

Remedy your tongue in my mouth, neutralize the pain
I will have to chain you up or push you out
Full entry—face-to-face
What does it take?
Because once you're in
you intend to possess my stomach
I felt it when I pulled you towards me
when we hit our limit I knew it was too much
but it was better than missing verse after verse after line
after incomprehensible emotion, spilled strategically,
pouring all over my pages

Sanity is overrated and those shakes you got are from years of
repression
write it out
It's building up and unrecognizable
Drawn on zero space—sideways with your tongue
WE
As far as my body will let you go
I grabbed your hands and before you could taste victory the lights came on
Like stopping a speeding train with those lips I was taken
It didn't hurt… more like a continuous dull ache
a reminder
It is everywhere you aren't

Forehead-to-forehead, three eyes staring back
I will have you transition from life to the supernatural
trade in all things rational
A reflection of myself taught to love
I'm still spinning
You swear it's worth every second of searching
So many layers
No shortcuts
Your lips on my navel pulling us through centuries of mapped out reconnaissance
Our bodies the only geographical location we sought out
Soul locked between lines of inverted compatibility
Never touching
Only synesthesia mixed with poetry, words lifting off pages
the sounds they make when I rearrange them
the colors that explode from my mouth as I speak them
We are no longer creating
we are being created

Secrets I Couldn't Keep

Erin Devlin

I LOST MY TRAIN OF thought, derailed car by car until the caboose flew over the cliff and couldn't be seen. Oma dissected my lie behind the penetrating gaze that she reserved for me alone. She didn't have to say anything. I couldn't stop talking. None of it was true, and she knew it by the end. I hadn't gone to the movies with Cindie Davis at 7:30pm the previous evening. We hadn't taken my car, and it hadn't run out of gas. We hadn't only had enough money for one cab ride, and we hadn't taken it to go to the Davis residence at 3567 Penbury Street. I hadn't tried to call Oma on her phone, and it hadn't gone to voicemail. After all the things that I told Oma that weren't true, I ended with one that was. I had spent the night at 3567 Penbury Street. Like the dirty carpets assumed to have always been gray, until you find a square of white carpet under the corner shelving, one true sentence exposed the fallacy. The train was on track until it wasn't.

Cindie Davis and I played on the high school basketball team together. She was the kind of girl who chewed gum loudly and spelled her name for everyone she met, even if they had no need to write it. I didn't dislike her. Her dad was one of our assistant coaches. He couldn't make it to many after school practices, but went out of his way to help us on the weekends. We would meet in the school gym, or sometimes at Cindie's house where they had a hoop set up in the driveway. When I pointed out to another teammate that Mr. Davis had an attractive way about him, she looked disgusted, and that was the last I said to anyone. I was one of the bigger girls, and I played power forward or center. Mr. Davis would wear basketball shorts and a t-shirt like the rest of us, and he would play too. He passed me the ball one evening and told me to dribble in for a basket. I bounced the ball back a few steps until my butt touched his leg, then turned and threw up a bad shot. He blocked it easily, and told me I had to make a better move than that. I tried again, starting at the base of the key and pivoting to square my hips toward him. The scent of his deodorant mixed with the smell of the sweat that had discolored the pits of his sleeveless brown t-shirt. I faked a shot and lunged around him with my left foot, planting it firmly and letting the force carry me toward the basket for an easy layup. I knew I had impressed him, but more, I knew I wasn't just a kid to him anymore. I knew that, but wouldn't have known how to say it out loud. It wasn't because of the layup.

Oma prodded me for the truth, and I let too much slip. She knew the right questions to ask, and she had enough experience in her life to know what seventeen-year-old girls can and will do. I wondered if she had ever done what I did, if back in Germany there had been a man she couldn't have, and if she decided that if she couldn't have him, she would at least destroy him.

I went to the drugstore after school one day and found myself in the deodorant aisle. Maybe I needed more deodorant. I pretended to look at the women's brands until the only other person in the aisle moved along, then I started to pick up the men's brands and smell them. They had names that evoked the Wild West and the Industrial Revolution, and they smelled like musty chemicals in the woods. When I found the right one, I bought it with my babysitting money and kept it under my pillow. On my restless nights, I brought it out and smelled it or rubbed it along my inner thigh. Something about doing that helped me fall asleep.

I drove past 3567 Penbury Street whenever I could or couldn't justify the detour. Mrs. Davis, her first name was Lisa, stayed at home during the days. According to Cindie, she worked on her Etsy business. She had bleached-blonde hair and a plastic surgery face, though I could never convince Cindie that her mom had gone under the knife. Cindie claimed Lisa's skin had always looked that unnaturally taut. I wondered what Lisa and Mr. Davis—his first name was Martin—talked about over dinner and in their bedroom. It must have been dull. Everything about my life that was interesting, and even some things that were not, I imagined telling to Martin. It would at least be less boring than whatever Mrs. Davis had to say about her Etsy business. She called him Marty, which I imagined he hated, but was too nice to mention. I wanted to call him Martin, but I always said Mr. Davis or Coach Davis because the other girls were around. He noticed me, and I could feel his eyes on my body. I flirted with him in ways that the other girls wouldn't notice. There was so much more to a grown man than to the boys at school. Those boys looked at me too, but their gazes at my chest were gross, and their sweat made their shirts cling to their thin torsos as they tried to show off in gym class. I made the mistake of kissing a particularly gangly one the year before, and had to feign an outburst of chastity when his tongue almost gagged me.

Oma threatened to go to the police, and I had to make her half a dozen promises before she agreed to at least wait a while. Oma was the most strong-willed person I knew, and she said the same about me. It was a characteristic of the Schmitz women, Oma said. Of the Schmitz men, and specifically of my father, she wouldn't speak. I was still technically in his custody, though the ten months after Mamá's death was the only period of time that I had seen him in my life, and the emotion of losing Mamá had wholly eviscerated me of any feelings that might have surfaced in response to his presence. Oma appeared with him and stayed with me, and from that moment she was my mother. Of her true child, the former missionary who had found a Guatemalan wife on a long-term mission trip and had brought her to the Pacific Northwest, only to abandon her and their baby daughter when he met another woman, she said nothing.

I knew that Lisa and Cindie would be gone for the night, because Cindie wouldn't shut up about the upcoming trip. By some miracle, she had been accepted to Seattle University, and they were visiting the city for a campus tour and information session. In the most casual voice I could muster, I asked Cindie if she could give me her dad's number, since I wanted to ask him about playing basketball in college. I was planning to attend the community college and thought I might have a chance. Cindie agreed right away, and told me how awesome it would be if I kept playing.

I didn't tell Martin how I had gotten his number or about wanting to play basketball in college, and he still invited me to his house. I told him I wanted to see him alone so we could really talk about things. He said I should come over at eight in the evening. I brought my makeup in my purse and put it on in the car, so Oma wouldn't see me wearing it when I left.

***

Martin gave me a hug and showed me into the house. It felt bigger without Cindie and our other teammates around me. I noticed some paintings for the first time. I told Martin about wanting to play basketball in college, and he asked me if I wanted to see his trophies from his college years. I nodded, and he led me to a side room I hadn't seen before with his hand on the small of my back. My hair was long, streaked red and blonde in a way that wasn't supposed to look natural, and braided down my back to where he was touching it, so that as he led me into the room it tugged lightly on my braid and I felt his touch all the way up on my head. Martin had played for a Division III team and won some sort of championship, though from what he was explaining it didn't sound like it was the most important one. I stood beside him and let my hand brush his side when I brought it up and down to point at the medals and trophies he had from high school and college sports.

He asked if I wanted to play a game of cards, and when I agreed we moved to the living room. He gave me the deck to shuffle and left the room. When he returned, he was holding two glasses of red wine. He handed one to me and made a toast to his basketball teams of the past and mine of the future. I looked into his eyes as I tried my first glass of red wine. The alcohols of my high school career were limited to cheap beer and cinnamon-flavored whiskey. I expected the taste of the wine to transport me to adulthood, to fill my palate with delicate hints of oak and apricot, but the wine tasted like stale juice and left an uncomfortable heat in the back of my throat. I drank the glass too fast, and Martin brought the bottle out to the table where we played Gin Rummy and laughed at nothing. I made him laugh so easily that I wondered if he was faking it. We finished the bottle of wine and he asked if we should open another. I felt woozy when I stood up to go to the bathroom, so I suggested we not, but when I returned to the table he had uncorked a bottle of rosé and filled my glass. The rosé tasted better, slightly less stale, and I tried hard not to drink too much from my glass. Martin had his hand on my thigh and was explaining his strategy for Gin Rummy. I asked if we could switch to a game I'd learned at summer camp, but I couldn't remember enough of the rules and suddenly Martin's face was close to my neck and the familiar scent of his deodorant reached my nose. It comforted me, in a way, and I made a move to stand up around him to get to a place I could breathe more easily. I didn't know if it was me who started kissing him, so when Oma asked who kissed who, I couldn't say for sure. The wine oozed through my mind and didn't let me think clearly, so I stopped thinking. I felt the stubble on his face and the easy sliding of my shirt up my arms. He didn't take me to his bedroom, but to the den where the Davis' had a futon for guests. Life's mystery faded. Thankfully he never asked if it was my first time.

I woke up on the futon alone at 3567 Penbury Street, covered from my shoulders to my knees with a throw blanket, needing to pee very badly. I was reaching around the room and finding pieces of clothing to put back on my body one by one, when I heard a car come up the driveway. Martin ran into the den, fully dressed, as I sat in my bra and cargo shorts with my shirt in my hand. I put my shirt in front of my chest automatically.

"Eva, you need to leave now," Martin said. I put my shirt on as he ushered me to the back door, his hand firmly on my shoulder and nearly pushing me. I told him I needed to pee, but he said to wait until I got home. I tried to make a joke, but he narrowed his eyes and didn't laugh. He whispered a barely audible goodbye as he shut the door on me. I thought I heard Lisa's voice in the entry hall, and it felt like a kick in the gut. I walked clear across the backyard, not attempting to hide. With the sound of the water in the fountain, the pressure in my bladder intensified, and I had an idea. I pulled my shorts down and squatted over the lowest tier of the fountain, peeing right into it as I mooned the Davis residence. My head throbbed with anger and a hangover, and my mouth tasted like dead mice, but at least I didn't have to pee anymore. I found out much later that Lisa had watched my whole encounter with the fountain. It came up in the divorce proceedings.

I didn't feel sorry for the Davis family. Martin turned out to be human or less, certainly not the man of my dreams, and I never cared for Lisa. Thinking about Cindie plucked a string of regret, but it was quickly stilled by the reassurance that she was too dumb to feel the damage in a real way. I did feel sorry for Oma, because she had me to deal with and I wasn't easy, but I was out of her gray hair soon. Our two families kept the secret well, so it must have been my imagination that my other classmates' mothers started giving me the stink-eye when I saw them in town, that they made sure to walk between me and their husbands in the streets. I always had a wild imagination.

Things Start At Their Names
John Sibley Williams

Ice locks the river in place and my heart
is static for the season and traversable.

Sometimes a boy about the age
my son would be adventures

halfway across me before remembering
the duty to destroy the one thing

beneath him. He writes his name
on my rib; it says *Curiosity*. I reply

with the name I've learned to wear:
Distance. A fluster of bluegill follows his body

downstream to where it meets the Columbia,
in time the ocean, which I cannot make freeze.

Next spring I will snare the things that still move in me,
beat them against stone, and eat until empty. I have

his name written all over my body; it says *Forever
be Winter*. My wife calls him *Gabriel*; after all these years

she still calls him *Gabriel*, and sometimes from the shore
she calls to me: *Thaw*.

Lost Family: FOUND!

Heather L. Nelson

(An Excerpt)

CHAPTER 10

I CONTINUED TO MULL OVER my mother's life and my own life as I waited for my brother, Kim, to make arrangements to get the letter scanned and emailed to me.

I felt I knew my mother very well. I've always felt close to her. I tried to honor her by planting the golden chain tree in her memorial garden. I also have a tribute grouping of photos of her life in my "family photo gallery" hanging on the wall in the upstairs hall. I grew melancholy as I thought of my mother. She will always live in my heart and memory, and I still miss her very much.

Finally, Kim called saying the letter was on its way. We continued to talk a few minutes, and then the letter appeared on my computer screen. Kim stayed on the line while I read the letter. The scan made the letters appear fuzzy, but readable. The letter said:

10th January 2013

Mr. Kim H Wheeler

Dear Mr. Wheeler:

I hope you may be able to help me. For some time now we have been working with Anthony to try to locate Heather Foster through the use of public records.

Sadly, we have recently discovered that Heather died in 2001.

Anthony was very sorry that he will not be able to contact Heather, however we noted that you are Heather's son.

I would therefore be very grateful if you would kindly telephone me so that we can discuss whether or not you would be willing to be in touch with Anthony who would welcome the opportunity to talk with you about Heather.

I am usually available most times, including early evenings. If you prefer you can write to me or email me.

I look forward to hearing from you.

Yours sincerely,
Hessie Edwards
AAA-NORCAP Intermediary

There was that name that Mom loved, *Anthony!* Somehow the memory of her mentioning that she loved the name jumped into my brain! I remembered the conversation she and I had had about the neighbor girl named Toni. I had been about nine years old at the time. Funny how I remembered that conversation through all the years.

I was very confused and a bit shocked! I told Kim I wanted to do a Google search on the agency to see if this letter was legitimate.

I found the letter was from an organization that helped put birth parents and adopted children in touch with each other. How could this possibly have anything to do with our mother?

World War II ended in England in May, 1945. Mom and Dad married April 25, 1946. I was born September 16, 1947. Kim was born April 11, 1949. I told Kim, "The only way I'll believe this could be a child of Mom's is if his birthdate is in late November or December of 1945, or possibly early January, 1946. Dad must have gone back to Bristol at the end of the war and left Mom pregnant right before he was shipped back to the states. Not knowing yet that she was pregnant, and not believing he would actually obtain a divorce from his American wife and send for her, she must have given up the child for adoption. Then when Dad made good on his word to send for her, she left England to come to the states and marry him, leaving the unmentioned baby adopted in England." This theory sounded a bit plausible, if uncharacteristic for our mother.

CHAPTER 11

Somehow, this unreal letter began to feel like it represented a real possibility. Kim and I discussed what we should do about it. Kim said, "Just send an email and see what they say." So I did.

The reply came back that the intermediary did not want to discuss this via email, and to please call or Skype. Kim decided to make the phone call.

Kim called me back after he contacted the agency. He had obtained a bit more information. The person looking for Mom was named Anthony Leonard, and he claimed to be her son. His birthdate was December 8, 1945. Kim obtained his email, phone number, and mailing address, and provided both our emails.

After several hours of agonizing disbelief and curiosity, I decided to send Anthony an email, introducing myself and forwarding some information about Mom: a picture of her and a memorial script from her funeral. I felt he had waited so long to know something about his mother—our mother. The idea still did not fully register with me.

Dear Anthony,

I can hardly believe I am writing to a brother I never even heard of before. My name is Heather Louann Nelson, your sixty-five-year-old sister. I always thought I was the oldest, with three younger brothers, Kim, Vance, and Barrie. I am sending you an article I wrote for our mother's memorial when she passed away in 2001. It tells a little bit about her life as I knew it.

I believe we have the same father too, because Harrison Wheeler was an American GI very much in love with Mom. When he shipped out probably at the end of the war (around May 1945) he may not have known you were on the way—Mom may only have had suspicions that she couldn't share during such an emotional time as the end of the war with Dad leaving. I knew it took her over a year to come to the USA, but she told me it took that long for Dad to come home, get settled, and earn enough money to send for her trip to the USA. During their separation, she may have had doubts that he would send for her at all.

Whatever the circumstances, I am sure it wrenched Mom's heart to part with you. She was such a kind person and had a great love for children.

I am also sending a picture that is a bit dark, but you can see how much in love Mom and Dad were. I am not sure when or where the picture was taken, whether in

England, or close to the time they got married. I will try to scan some other pictures to send to you. This picture is one I happened to have on my computer already.

I am anxious to hear about your life. I hope you have had wonderful parents and a happy upbringing. Please let us know how you are doing, and tell us about your family and life in general.

I know that both Kim and I have been through a range of emotions hearing the news that we have a new brother. Wow! Still can't believe it! But welcome to the family! Looking forward to hearing from you and maybe eventually meeting you someday.

Love,
Your sister Louann

On January 20, 2013, I got the following email letter from the brother I had never heard from before:

Hello Heather Louann:

I, too, cannot believe I am contacting a blood-related relative so far away. I am on an emotional 'roller coaster' and pinching myself that this is all happening! First of all, I want to sincerely thank you for sending the initial information regarding our mother. The memorial script conveniently condenses the life story of 'mom', of which I found completely fascinating. Of course there are lots of questions I would like to ask and find answers to which I am sure you will understand.

The impact for me to see a photograph of my birth mother for the first time was emotionally overwhelming. I am pleased to know that she was likeable and well respected and best of all a lovable person. I am grateful I have come from a good pedigree! I am hesitant to accept that Harrison Wheeler is my father at the moment but when you see the photograph of me you will be able to make a judgment. If there is any uncertainty then I would be prepared to have a DNA test undertaken.

There is so much to say, I think it best that I forward a mini biography of myself when I have a calmer moment. I will give a potted diary of my life just for now.

I was adopted by Thomas and Mary Leonard. 'Dad' was invalided out of the home guard as far as I can tell but was always a farm worker. Mum was a munitions worker for the war effort, married circa 1943. Mum had trouble in being able to conceive, so adopting "little me" was the answer. It was a private adoption (I have all the paper trail for this including two letters from 'Mom').

By this time it seems that as a family we led a pretty transient lifestyle, moving around to different farms, mainly in the county of Sussex (south of London).

But bingo! My influence on home life created five brothers for me! There were two girls born but unfortunately both developed complications and did not survive.

Reflecting on my home life, I found the frequent moving from farm to farm in different parts of the south of England upsetting. Getting use to new schools I detested, but once settled in I actually enjoyed doing my best at schoolwork. At secondary level, I became interested in art, science and geography, found maths (arithmetic in those days!) difficult!

I perhaps did not 'gel' towards my brothers, especially the older ones, we seem to be on a war footing for most of the time. I really did feel different from the rest of the family. My outlook and aptitude seem to be above everybody else and I had a general disdain for my dad. For, as I headed towards my teens, I thought he was irresponsible for the way the household was managed and for the apparent never ending relocations (each house was generally a farm cottage—some didn't even have electricity up until about 1960). Mum was very subservient to him. (Both parents passed away some years ago).

I did enjoy the rough and tumble of the freedom of the fields, being able to go anywhere on exploration sprees, something that youngsters are restricted to doing today.

Although I wanted to stay on at school, to get some school certificates, I had no choice as I was emphatically told that my parents could not afford to keep me at school so I left when I was fifteen years old.

For a while I worked with my Dad on the same farm. Fortunately, a previous employer had seen my dad advertising for another job and offered to give me responsibility to help run a dairy herd of cows. In the package was agricultural training (going to college one day a week). I loved the job and excelled at what I did generally. I also learnt to be independent and make my own decisions.

Moving on—the opportunity was presented to me about studying General Agriculture at College in Hampshire (Near Winchester). I qualified and was recommended to study agricultural engineering and farm mechanization. Off I went to a College in Sussex (Near Lewes).

Now qualified in farm machinery maintenance, I worked at a government agricultural research institute (near Maidenhead), and was responsible for the upkeep of a wide range of farm equipment.

I then returned to Sussex to work as the workshop senior technician, responsible for staffing and running the whole college workshop including tractors, vehicles, welding and blacksmith provisions. I met Kate, the College farm's shepherd (who had a sheepdog 'Meg'). We moved to where we are now, Market Weighton—about twenty-five miles east of York in the north of England. Kate and I got married within the year in 1986.

I had taken a lecturing post at a College near Beverley, teaching welding and farm mechanization. After about sixteen years service, I resigned and went into fabrication and welding for two-plus years. I was made redundant and then was offered a post at the previous College as an assessor in agricultural engineering, working with trainees (apprentices). I did this for eight years and then decided to ease off the pressures of life and left to work in the technology department of a boys secondary school in Beverley, as the technician, I keep the department running smoothly (most of the time!) doing maintenance and preparing materials etc.

So I keep myself busy, but I keep threatening to retire from regular work, this is something I need to think about.

From the above, you can get an idea of my life's experience to date.

I ought to mention our two children before I go! (I love them to bits!) Catherine Anna (I would like you to know that I had chosen Heather as the first name but got out voted!) is now twenty-five and single. She has recently got a new job as an ecologist with the Environment Agency, a government organization. Catherine's a specialist in rivers and water course environments. She works from Chichester in Sussex.

Richard Anthony, coming up to nineteen, is doing trombone studies at the Royal Conservatoire of Scotland in Glasgow. Richard is in his second year of the four-year course and is quite an accomplished trombonist. Richard does not have any of my genes for music, but Kate is quite musical and likes singing!

As I said, there is a lot to tell but I'm sure as we keep in touch the rich tapestry of each other's lives will be revealed in time. I have included some photos for you. I think in time I will be able to scan some childhood photos—none of me as a tiny tot!

Will sign off now.

With love and best wishes,
Your brother Anthony

PS. Sorry to knock you off the number one spot!

CHAPTER 12

I stared at Anthony's picture. I saw a familiar face, full of family resemblance: Mom's smile, Dad's thick, wavy, sandy-salt-and-pepper hair, Kim's brown eyes and big ears, Barrie's nose. He did not have the dimple in his chin as Dad, Kim, and Barrie did. Nevertheless, he looked so familiar, it was uncanny. He had had a life of moving around and attending many different schools too, just like we did! Our upbringings were not so very different! I replied back right away!

Hello Big Brother,

I am still trying to get used to you. I definitely see a lot of family resemblance with you, Kim, and Barrie. You have brown eyes like Kim, the rest of us have blue-gray like Mom and Dad. You have the same big ears like we all do. Mom's trait. Your nose looks more like Barrie's. The rest of us have bigger noses. You have Mom's mouth and teeth. You definitely have the look of my other brothers. It could be that you have Dad's hair and forehead. It is so uncanny to see your picture.

I am so glad to know you have a wonderful wife and children! They are very beautiful and precious! I am happy to have a new sister-in-law and a niece and nephew. Unreal. I have three sons, Paul, Jason, and Jared, all married with families. I too, have a wonderful husband, Brian. He is also sixty-seven, but his birthday is in February. We have five grandkids, and one more grandson on the way, due March 31. Kim has no kids, but has a long-term girlfriend, Emily. Vance (his childhood nickname which I still call him is Buster) is married to Shirley who is from Brazil and they have one daughter Vanessa (very musical) who is getting her masters in music back East. Barrie is married to Sue and they have four kids—two boys, Eric and Scott, and two girls, Kristin and Heidi. Three are out of college and one just started. We are all scattered across the western part of the states. I'm in Oregon, Kim and Jason are in Nevada, Vance is in California, and Barrie is in Arizona. My oldest son, Paul, is in New Mexico. And now you are over in England!

I went to England with my mother when I was twelve years old. At that time, there were other family still alive to visit. You would've been fourteen. Barrie went over with Mom, too, in the mid '60s when he was a young boy. I believe she went over after we were grown again, with Sam, her second husband. By the way, he is still alive, I think he is ninety-one now. He lives in the same house as he did with Mom in Nevada, close to Kim.

Can you sing? Mom had a most beautiful soprano voice. I didn't inherit it. Barrie can sing well, but he is the only one.

As far as professions go: I retired two-and-a-half years ago after twenty-five years working in hospital administration and support services. No, I did not become a nurse like Mom. As a hobby I like to write children's stories for my grandkids. Since retirement I have published a children's book, "Daisy the Protector Dog." You might be able to find it in England. I'm not sure, but it is supposed to be available in English speaking countries. I am working on a second book for teens, "First Summer with Horses." I hope to publish it this year. Kim worked in the casinos in Reno and was almost a semi-pro tennis player in his younger days. He is retired now and takes a lot of cruises these days, with an elderly lady friend. Barrie works in the computer industry (as does my second son, Jason), and Vance is in the restaurant business.

I am attaching a few pictures. The first one is of Barrie. He flies his own plane. He and I have our paternal grandmother's white hair. Kim still has brown hair. I think Vance is getting a bit gray, more like yours. The second picture is of me with two of my grandkids, both four years old, Bradley (Jared's son) and Maria (Jason's daughter). We are riding Lupita, one of my horses (I have five horses at present; we rescued three of them last summer). The third picture is of Kim and me. I haven't got any scanned pictures of Vance except some when he was younger that he emailed me. I will try to get some more recent pictures from him.

And that leads to telling both Barrie and Vance about you. Barrie is the baby of the family and doted on by Mom. He will have a very hard time with this. Mom can do no wrong in his eyes. Vance will also have a hard time. He will probably believe a DNA test but nothing less. These are my speculations, of course, but I feel they will both be thoroughly in shock. I will talk to Kim about the best way to break the news.

Sorry I have been very disjointed in writing this email. I have so many questions for you. What is your middle name? How tall are you? You say you have two letters from Mom? I would love if you would share them with me. The fact that you are mechanical and a country-loving guy fits right in with the type of person Dad was, and Mom was very artistic, so you inherited traits from both of them. I am going to go through some old papers/pictures in a suitcase that I have of Mom's to see if there is any information about when Dad actually left England, when he was discharged from the Army, and whatever else I might find that might be pertinent.

I am so happy you wrote back and told me a little about your life. I know Kim wants to know all this, so I will probably forward this to him. If you don't mind. I hope your wife, Kate, is willing to share you with your American relatives. We might overwhelm you both at first, until all this settles down, if it ever does.

So happy to have you for a brother!

Love,
Your sister Louann

And so Anthony, Kim, and I began to get acquainted as brothers and sister at sixty-seven, sixty-five, and sixty-three years of age.

An Ordinary Thing
Susan Sweetland Garay

Walking from the grocery store
to the car with a cart full of groceries,
a baby strapped to my chest.

Such an ordinary thing. I do not
expect to be surprised by
something beautiful.

But that is exactly what happens.

A swirl of petals,
fallen from a tree full of
springtime blooms,
turn in a perfect circle
in the air.

Floating higher
and higher.

A small cyclone.
A tornado of petals
swirling against
the two-toned
grey of sky
and pavement.

A spot of life in a parking lot.
A fleeting, windblown
work of art.

A La Carte
Lynn Blatter

THE FAMILIAR NEIGHBORHOOD SOUNDS WERE magnified by a clear, crisp October evening in the vicinity of the Molalla Historical Society. Families were going about their evening routines, dogs called out to each other, and cars with tired commuters arrived home.

A night watchman was on-site at the Von der Ahe house as renovations to the foundation were underway, and materials and tools scattered the area. Hourly, the guard came out of his office trailer to make rounds, stopping to survey jet-black surroundings. This evening, a noise by the summer kitchen caught his attention. He followed the flagstone path by the cupola and, step-by-step, insidious fear welled up. Something was out there. His years of security experience gave him a sixth sense about unusual situations. He slowed as he approached the fenced area, hand on his radio. EEEEEK!! Wings whizzed by him as a body brushed his leg. His heart pounded with terror. He quickly realized a bat had flown from the rafters and scared a stray cat into flight. He exhaled the breath he'd been unconsciously holding. Both bat and cat disappeared into the dark. Relief elicited a quiet chuckle. He was on edge; the curator had warned him of some strange occurrences since the repairs had begun.

Suddenly, the security lights blinked out. He stopped, waiting for the battery backups to kick in. There were absolutely no lights or sounds in the surrounding homes and streets. Seconds passed, but it remained dark. The cold increased rapidly, working its fingers through his thick jacket. A viscous fog descended, limiting visibility to the end of his fingers.

"Unit one to base. Unit one to base. Come in base." Not even a crackle of static broke the eerie quiet. "Base, come in!" The green light on the radio unexpectedly blinked out. He turned to go back to the trailer to replace the battery.

Passing the cupola, the sound of children's voices and laughter broke the peace. A strange glow showed from the windows of Ivor Davies Hall, and he realized the antique chandeliers from the old high school were glimmering through the glass. Were those drumbeats coming from the street? He moved toward the sound, stopping to stare at the brick column with the Indian shield throbbing to the drum cadence. Freezing bands of horror began to bind his chest, and his nerves jumped and crawled like spiders. Never in his long career of police work had he felt such fright. Gong! He whirled around to see the school bell opposite the Indian swinging as though an invisible hand was issuing a summons to class. He stood glued to the spot. Gulping down much needed air, he summoned the courage to sprint toward the safety of his office, but he lost his footing on the uneven turf and fell at the base of the cupola. He dragged himself onto the bench surrounding the structure to catch his breath and calm down. It was not to be.

Sinewy, slimy tendrils emerged from between the bench slats and slid around him. With unearthly strength, they pulled him backward into the cupola as his screams echoed against the buildings. Silence resumed, the dense fog instantly disappeared, and sounds of cars and televisions could be heard again. The most chilling sounds, however, were heard coming from the cupola—a child's evil sounding giggle and… a burp!

Don't Mistake Tenderness For Weakness
Kate Gray

IF YOU REALLY WANT TO tell your story, you shouldn't teach, honest to God, and besides, students don't want to hear a middle-aged professor drone on about his sad sack of a life. You may think that by telling them, you'll spare them something awful because you're that kind of guy, but when it comes right down to it, keep it to yourself.

That's what you should've done, but you didn't.

At Clark Kent Community College—no kidding, a college named by someone obsessed with Superman—you're the kind of teacher that puts students in small groups, kneels beside them when reviewing their thesis statements, actually gives a shit. At least according to what students write on Rate My Professors sometimes. Never a chili pepper. Your students think you're too geeky since your glasses are round like John Lennon's and your hair's parted in the middle. Button-down cotton shirts tucked into jeans and a belt don't yell sexy. Who rates a professor according to hotness anyway?

So, you should have known from the start of class that it was going to tank. When you were passing out blank sticky notes for students to write down their thesis statements, one note slapped on each rough draft, four rough drafts to a table, and the third sticky had *DickButt* printed in pencil on it, and everyone at the table read it before you crumpled it in your sun-spotted hand, the day could do nothing but go to hell.

DickButt could have been some Holden Caulfield moment, but you'd taken the yellow sticky notes from the supply cabinet in the department workroom. Someone in some other class must have written *DickButt* four stickies in and returned the pad to some instructor, and that instructor returned the notes to the cabinet. Lucky you.

The three girls at the table, all twenty-somethings with their blond hair in ponytails, jerked their heads back from the table and, you swear, took in their breath like three elephants sucking water from a trough. The fourth person at the table was more thirty-something and had tattoos down both arms, the swirly kind with reds and teal, and he was doodling on his paper that had one sentence and no paragraph. His pencil carved into the paper a big rose. The rose had raindrops between the petals, little ones, and with the collective gasp and the crumpling note, you leaned

Cold Night, Little Owl
Larry Anderson

I hear noise, walk to the fireplace. A wing twisted, a foot clawing
the chimney wall, an owl the size of my fist has fallen
into the corner of the grate. He sits, aflame.

Smoke of singed feathers drifts from the fireplace. I recoil,
retreat, into fear and dread.

I can't move. What words work? Who understands this? I
scream for help in an empty house.

I must move in clarity, not in halting,
flaming, instants.

Gingerly, quickly, I act.

Outside, he dies smoldering in my gloved hands.

I kneel in the autumn leaves and weep.

toward the drawing, and that's when you saw the scream in each drop, Edvard Munch's scream-face in each little drop.

"Just write your thesis statement on the sticky," you said. And whoever named those notes sticky must not have been a man. A man would have named them something understated and staccato, the sound of the word so damn soft and effeminate, and a man with tattoos who drew roses with screaming raindrops doesn't question words and probably says sticky without questioning himself.

You put a blank sticky on James's paper and knelt beside him.

"Good save," James said. He gave you a wink like the two of you knew each other from the gym or something.

"Nice drawing," you said and pointed at the rose, "How about a thesis statement?"

He shrugged.

"Come to my office hour after class," you said and got up despite your knees. Then you worried about what else might be written in the stickies when you stuck them on the rest of the papers.

But James did come to your office hour. When he entered your office, you thought a crowd walked in. His leather smell mixed with tobacco told something truer than *Moby Dick*, the book you couldn't bring yourself to read again, but your mother had bound for you when you finished your PhD. You didn't do your PhD on *Moby Dick*, but it was her favorite book.

James had written a total of ten sentences since the beginning of WR 95, a developmental writing course that was supposed to help students connect sentences into paragraphs. For each of the five assignments, he turned in two sentences. The two-sentence paragraphs generally had to do with baking. Waking up for class after the graveyard shift at Kettleman's Bagels with the only boiled bagels in Portland, he stretched out in the undersized chairs, plastic and cheap, furniture the college bought in the '90s, orange chairs you hoped would reveal another identity and supersize themselves, but they didn't. James stretched his legs out in the classroom and rested his massive arms on the table, his forearms all muscle and tattoo, showing the way he rolled and shaped dough and turned doughnuts into perfect boiled bagels, crisp on the outside and malty and chewy on the inside. Chewy is another one of those words.

"Getting enough sleep?" you said.

"Plenty," he said.

Why you expected more than one word from him was a lot like chasing a whale in a sailing ship.

"Sorry about the sticky note."

"It sucks, doesn't it?" he said. He hadn't shaved in a few days, and the smile he gave you made the dark part of his cheeks move.

"Oh God, not at all." You raised your hands like you were saying *Stop,* like you wanted him to stop thinking that.

"My writing sucks. I know."

"No, really," you said.

"No, really," he said.

It did suck, but that wasn't the point. You asked him about baking, and what he wanted to do with college. And he told you about his grandfather baking bread in Nebraska and getting to work someplace besides in the cornfields, and later, his grandfather raising him in Eagle Creek, Oregon, where he milled his own timber, and the two of them were all they had. And he told you about his girlfriend, how she wants to write, but he's the one taking a writing class. She reads dark novels by crazy writers, like Something Plath and Joyce Carol Something. And he asked you why you write since he knew you wrote poetry because his girlfriend wants to write something she calls savage, something so harsh and violent that people will know what life dishes out.

"She's been through a lot," he said. "Tried to kill herself with a shotgun blast through the gut. But she woke up. Spent months in rehab. Can't digest right."

"Ouch," you said. And nothing you could say would be the right thing to say.

"Maybe she could talk with you."

And nothing you could say would make her life right. You said, "Sure."

And if you think back on what happened, you should have said something else.

"I got this for her," he said, and he stood up so quickly in your little office, you had to lean back in your chair. James turned around and lifted up the back of his tee shirt exposing his skin. One big tattoo covered his back with writing like you saw on bearded men riding Harleys. It said, *Don't Mistake Tenderness For Weakness.* The lettering on his skin was thick and script and intricate. "She's been with a lot of bad guys, you know. Beat the crap out of her. She takes meds because her chemistry's screwed up, but for now, she's off them, trying to make her head right. She wants me strong, not wrong."

With that slogan you couldn't help but think of all the students who came to your office and rattled off the Big Book: *it works if you work it, keep coming back, one day at a time*. At Clark Kent Community College students showed up for class with cellophane between who they were in front of you and everything they were outside of class, the things inside them that threatened to burst through. You could see the strain and bubbles of the transparent film barely holding them together, and for James, he was trying to hold together two people. You knew that he had two people's pain carved into his skin. And even more painful was knowing he was an artist, someone who could take on what other people felt and feel it so deeply, he could mix it inside himself, and make it beautiful. He was someone who turned loneliness and terror into raindrops between rose petals. When he put his shirt back down, you thought, *easy does it*.

Maybe your eyes were cellophane. They filled and stretched to spilling. Something about a man trying to make up for the wrongs done to a woman stuck a plug in your throat. Your breathing got fast and shallow.

"iProf, you Okay?" All the students called you that since your last name was Apple. James looked at you like he might call 9-1-1.

"Fine," you said. "It's that sticky note and how badly I feel about it." And when you got flustered, song tracks went off in your head, like "Heart of Gold," all high and whiny, and you started talking, and pretty soon you told James about each of your wives, how both of them had been students, the way they looked at you like you were the first novel they had ever read, and for a few years after they graduated and you married, you shared words and cooking and rides to the grocery store. You were that kind of husband. But when it was over and you lost the houses, they said they never felt equal even though you put their names on everything, paid for their BAs, hyphenated your last names. They said you used your power over them. They left you for men their own age, and you heard from colleagues about their marriages and children and advanced degrees. And you drank and drank until the pain was in the resistance to pain. You went to AA. And it wasn't until you told James about your cat, his way of sitting at the window like a great horned owl, which is why you named him Archimedes after Merlin's talking owl in *The Sword in the Stone*, your favorite novel which your mom hated, and Archi's the only thing that talks to you in your condo, that you realized you'd been talking.

"Damn, iProf, sorry," he said, and what you should tattoo on your back came clear to you with James filling up the office: *Don't Mistake Talking for Teaching* in thick cursive. Teachers at a community college aren't supposed to show students the cellophane holding their insides in.

For the second time you apologized to him, and you figured you ought to do something nice.

"How about the three of us have coffee?"

"Really?" James said. "You would?" He stroked the beard growing on his cheek.

"Sure."

"How about Trails Inn at three tomorrow? My girl waits tables and gets off her shift then, and we could meet you."

"In Estacada?"

"We live on my opa's land a few miles out. We'll meet you then."

On the drive the next day to the Trails Inn Café and Timber Room in Estacada, the curves came too fast in your old Honda Civic. The cedars along the river crowded out the light, and even though you knew Ray Carver didn't grow up there, you could see him scaling trees, using words like *ballhooter* and *choker hooks*. Teaching students who lost their jobs when the timber industry tanked meant reading paragraphs filled with longing, for ways that men used to use their arms, for things they did together that made a difference to their wives. James and his opa from Nebraska used to take down these trees. Driving to Estacada, honest to God, was like driving into another century, one with homesteaders and feuding cousins and old women with shotguns in their laps rocking chairs on the front porch. Everyone in Estacada knew guns and lumber grades and pickup trucks.

The Trails Inn Café and Timber Room wasn't hard to find, and before walking in, your nose plugged with smoke, and your gait slowed so you could catch your breath. Maybe restaurants in Estacada didn't have to be non-smoking like those in the rest of Oregon. You didn't mind so much since every AA meeting started with smoke from everybody nervous and lighting up outside.

James stood up from a small table in the back.

"iProf, thanks for coming. This'll mean a lot to her."

"My pleasure," you said. "Where's your girlfriend?"

"Marian just texted. She had to pick something up after work. She'll be back here in a minute."

The waitress in jeans and a cutoff top that showed her white belly came to ask what drinks you wanted, and not bothering to ask if they made lattes, you ordered coffee black, and so did James.

"Have you been drawing a long time?" you said after the mug of coffee arrived and coffee splashed on the table, and the waitress didn't wipe it up. James said you should try the maple bars because the ones made here were the best in the world.

And then he said, "I've been doodling as long as I can remember."

"You're really good," you said and tried to look him in the eye so he'd know you weren't saying something you'd apologize for later. "You should take art classes."

"What for?" he said. "Can't make a living by doodling." The mug was small between his hands.

Neither of you saw Marian until she was standing by the table. She was skinny, swear to God, like a tree limb is skinny when it's dead and sticking out, the bark fallen off, and even from a few feet away, the cut marks on the inside of her arms made stripes. Women in my classes who wrote about cutting said they cut themselves where nobody could see the marks, and you knew what James told you was understated and true. Marian had it rough. Even James might not know how rough Marian had it.

"Hey," James said to Marian, "you made it."

"Fuck," Marian said and didn't sit down. Her legs in tight jeans looked like they could snap any minute.

"What's the matter?" James said. He stood up and reached for her shoulder.

She jumped away from his hand. "Fuck, fuck, fuck," she said, and both her hands shot up to her forehead, and she spun around, and that made her elbows go out, and she looked like a beater blade of a blender turning round and round. "I can't believe he's here."

Beyond the truth that you were no chili pepper, you didn't know how to take this. Before you, in the flesh, was the scream that the raindrops contained. Here was the rose that only James could turn into more blossom than thorn. His reason for drawing, for going back to school, for two-sentence paragraphs was twitching in front of you.

"Glad to meet you," you said, and you weren't, but that wasn't the point. James wanted something from you, and his tenderness was worth a drive to Estacada, a talk with a twitchy girl. Marian looked at the hand you extended until you put it down.

"How about we sit," James said. And the three of you sat, but Marian looked at the coffee mugs, the window, the walls. Her legs jumped like jackhammers. The waitress returned with two maple bars, said hello to Marian who didn't say hello back.

The maple bars smelled so sweet they almost crunched. When you picked one up, it was moist between your fingers. You had it almost to your mouth when Marian yelled, "Don't eat that!" and her hand slapped the maple bar across the room.

"Marian!" James said.

The Trails Inn Café went silent, and the other customers stared at the maple bar on the wood floor and then at Marian and then at you.

"Fuck it," she said, and she stuck her hand in the pocket of her raincoat and leaned across the table. "I want you to listen to me, DickButt, listen close. We're going to walk out of here and get into James's truck, and you're not going to make a sound." From the hand in the pocket, from the bulge of it, you were going to do what she said.

"What the fuck?" James said.

"Shut up, James."

You swear to God you thought you were in a movie. Cameras and lights must have been somewhere, but you didn't see them. And since you were that kind of customer, the kind that doesn't stiff a waitress, you reached for your wallet. Marian spun toward you with her hand pointing the thing in her pocket, but then she saw and said, "Okay." So, you left your only cash, a twenty, and the three of you walked out of the Trails Inn Café in a line, you first, then James, then Marian. James took the lead to the truck, and Marian said, "Get in James. iProf in the middle, don't try anything." And you did what she wanted you to do. "Drive the old reservoir road, James." He started the truck, backed out of the lot, and pulled on to the road.

"What the fuck are you doing, Marian?" He pulled himself toward the windshield and tried to look two places at once. Sitting in the middle over the engine, you blocked most of what he could see of her. She leaned against the door a little to keep an eye on both of you.

"You'll see," she said. And she drew her hand out of her raincoat, and in it was a .38 Special, something you had seen only in movies, but up close, honestly, it was something beautiful and animal and so awful it clogged your throat. There it was, the black barrel and the wood handle and the curve that fit her hand. You didn't know enough about guns to see a safety, on or not, or anything except how the revolver seemed muscular like a shark. Your breath got short.

"Calm down, iProf," James said.

"Can't," you said, "breathe."

James pulled over. On the old reservoir road the pavement was all ruts, and, you realized, ever since the highway bypass went in, nobody went there anymore.

"Not here," Marian said.

"We have to," James said. "iProf can't breathe." He opened the door and slid off the bench seat. Before he took another step, Marian opened her door and faced you with the gun.

"Get out, DickButt." You slid toward her to get out the door. Your hands were in the air in case she thought you might do something. There was nothing you could think of doing, your mind running through the last day, through colleagues who might live out this far, through stories with bad endings. As soon as your feet hit the ground, you doubled over like somebody who finished a race and tried to catch his breath except your knees were too bad to run.

"Hands up," she said and touched the gun to your back. "That'll help you breathe." And when you raised your hands, your lungs cleared, and you really could, believe it or not, breathe better.

"What's going on, Marian?" James said. He was on your left, the two of you facing her.

"Fuck, James, fuck," she said. "How could he do that to you?"

"Do what?"

"How could he call your writing something so bad?"

"What're you talking about?" James said. She pointed the gun at him. His hands shot in the air, and he backed away. "Easy," he said.

"He wrote it on the Post-it Note and stuck it to your writing. Your writing. Your writing. Something you created. How could he?" Any time she said the word *he*, she jabbed the revolver at you.

"That's not what he meant."

"Isn't it?"

"No," you said, "mistake." Each word took one whole breath.

"Shut up," she said and aimed the gun higher, at your face. Her hands were shaking, and she leaned on one foot, then the other.

"Tell me this, Mr. Professor Apple. Do you believe that all writers must suffer something savage in order to write something lasting?"

Marian's face had the shape of your ex-wives' faces, and you knew very clearly that, just like they said, you had used your power over them. You were sorry, just like that.

"Not necessarily," you said.

"Wrong answer," she said. And the gun popped, and a bullet hit a tree fifty feet away with a thud. "Think before you speak." The gun had recoiled, but she handled it. With nothing to her arms but bone, nothing to her face but flesh, she knew guns the way someone does who does whatever they have to do to live. All you could see was the black barrel, the shine of it, the curve. Honest to God, the eye of the gun was looking into your eyes, and what it saw was nothing. You were that kind of scared.

"Marian, listen to me," James said, "iProf didn't mean it. A kid wrote that note and stuck it back, and iProf didn't know it was there."

"How do you know?"

"He told me."

"And you believed him," she said. "How many times do I have to tell you? Don't you listen to me? You can't believe what people say, James." And she spread her feet, took the gun in both hands. "Next question."

"Cut it out, Marian," James said. "Stop." He stepped toward her.

"Back off," she said. And she aimed the gun at his chest. The revolver was in both her hands, which were steady for the first time.

And James kept coming.

And she fired the gun, and the pop sounded fake, but James spun, and he fell, and blood poured out of his chest.

"Oh my God," she said, "Oh my God. James." And she ran to him, and stood over him, and both of his hands were on his chest, and the blood was pumping between his fingers, and when she kneeled down beside him, she put her hand on his chest and said, "James? James?" He tried to pick his head up, and she leaned toward him and said so softly, "Don't."

And she said so softly, "I'm sorry."

And when she lifted the gun to her mouth, stuck it in, and pulled the trigger, you said, "Wait," but it happened too fast.

You've read about moments after moments like these, that there's some weird quiet, some way that the cedar branches sway, and peace fills the gap left by violence. But that's not this story. In this story there was no silence. James yelled, and his chest made sucking sounds, and 9-1-1 kept you talking, and you rolled your shirt into a ball and pressed it into the hole in James's chest, and sirens filled up the reservoir, and men in uniforms made you move out of the way. The gurney clicked when they raised it, and the doors to the ambulance slammed, and the sirens echoed through the hills when they took James away.

You've wanted to tell this story, but if you did, you'd hear "Stairway to Heaven" or some '70s song and start missing the students you don't teach anymore, the ones who couldn't connect sentences into paragraphs, the ones who couldn't figure out how to wrap parts of themselves up in cellophane and keep those out of class. When you reach into your jeans' pocket and finger that year's AA coin, you think about telling your story in some meeting, but you don't. You don't tell your story even though it might help somebody because that's not your job anymore.

Definitions
Sandra Rokoff-Lizut

Hope—
slowly flickers till its last bit
of strength is spent.

We are then released to morn
         released to heal
         released to stumble upon
                  a course not contemplated
                  before hope blocked our entry.

Time—
the lover, lures us back
into bliss
bids us to live there forever

the thief, filches our youth
and that of our children

the parent, drags us
snotty-nosed and blubbering,
forward

the elephant, tethered
to today's minutia
staggers round
      and round
            and round

The Big World
John Flavin
(An Excerpt)

The narrator of the story—Neither Nor Johnson, Director of Limbo—explains why he is about to take his readers on a tour of the one, real afterworld.

Neither-Nor Johnson, Director of Limbo:

God has determined that this whole Apocalypse thing really isn't necessary at all. Officially, he didn't make a mistake; he changed his mind. You see, the problem with allowing Satan to burn the Earth and punish sinners forever is that, unlike here in the Afterworld, you mortal sinners after the Apocalypse would get no chance for redemption. If you get caught red-handed being sinful at the turn of the twentieth century—you know, stabbing someone for money or raping your kid—and Satan gets loosed upon the Earth, that's it, you're done for. No redemption. No saying, "I didn't mean it!"

That's the nice thing about the Afterworld, you can always be redeemed. God always Forgives.

Let me tell you a little story. One time, you see, a baby was born. And when that baby was born, so was Love. Though it's true that people have always fallen in Love, wrestled with Love, and some have even hated It, because, unrequited, Love kind of sucks. But experiencing Love sensations and Affirming Love through one's Faith in God, well, they are two entirely different things.

And then there was Jesus, the baby, the boy: a walking, living, breathing embodiment of Love's Affirmation through Faith in God. Muhammad? Same deal, but he never really had the same impact on people because of the unfortunate sequel-effect; sequels are rarely as captivating as the original. It's all timing. Anyway, the story goes that Satan saw God's spontaneous little offspring spreading this Passion throughout the land, and he could see that the people were gobbling up His Word like chocolate.

Well, just as I had predicted—although no one wants to admit it—Satan wanted his share of the fun, too. He turned to God, after observing Jesus for a while, and said with remarkable composure, "I want to be among the mortals, too. It's not fair that Jesus gets to and I don't! It's not fair!" Satan was jealous of the new baby in the family, and God did the Honorable thing. He recognized that Satan was absolutely right.

> *"But the cowardly, the unbelieving, the vile, the murderers, the sexually immoral, those who practice magic arts, the idolaters and all liars— they will be consigned to the fiery lake of burning sulfur. This is the second death."*
> ~~Revelation 21:8

It was not fair at all that Jesus got to walk among the mortals, and not Satan, and He turned to the little horned fellow, and said, "How right you are, young'un. I will give you that opportunity as well, and it will be a thousand years thus. A thousand years from this day, you will be loosed upon the Earth and you shall wreak havoc on all the sinners in whatever manner you see fit; come the next millennium, Satan, you shall punish sinners directly. The tiny watery planet will be yours to set aflame."

If ya ask me, He was letting Satan do His dirty work.

Satan held his hands under his chin and he curled and mingled his fingers together. With a great big smile, eyes wide and fixed on nothing in particular, and without moving his lips, he uttered, "Really? Little ole me?"

He snarled for a short while over the issue of having to wait a thousand years. But Satan bided his time and before long, around 476 CE, he began gathering heat from below the Earth's surface and doing trial re-runs with great volcanic blasts and burning whole towns and villages. He even tried firing up a few bags of cats just to see what sound effect he might get. By 999 CE, Satan was ready. The rivers would scald gorges into the ground; the rain would melt everything; the sun would burn holes into flesh; the water supply would all be polluted with toxins; whole plant and animal species would vanish. The world of sinners would suffer eternal damnation by the direct command of Satan.

Just as we all had been promised!

But then suddenly, God came to him right as he prepared to pounce. He said, "Satan?"

Distracted and annoyed, Satan looked up to God and said, "God?"

God said, "If you wait to be loosed upon the Earth toward the end of the *second* millennium, two thousand years after the second rising of My Son, there will be an explosion."

But he said no more. That was all. Satan pleaded with God to tell him what kind of explosion would take place, or what it meant. But God offered no reply. He simply folded his arms in Holy defiance. But Satan is a clever fellow, and he knew God wouldn't bother him right at that very moment for some petty explosion. He had nearly six mortal hours—until sunrise—in the first day of the second millennium of Jesus' birth (1033 CE; 6:29 a.m., to be exact) to determine the meaning of God's riddle. He paced back and forth, mulled it over, and then amputated and castrated a few demons in chaotic frustration.

"What does it mean? Damn His mysterious ways!"

Suddenly, Satan's prehistoric intuition offered advice, as if a miniature version of himself sat upon his own shoulder, whispering, "Go with it. Wait until millennium number two." Satan obeyed the miniature version of himself and though he didn't know it at the time, his gamble paid off dearly: the explosion God foresaw was the population explosion.

It took Satan until the year 1811 to realize that he had not been fooled; the number of people on earth had gone from well below one billion to well over that. The advancements in medicine led to seven billion potential sinners in 2011, just twenty-two wee years before the second millennium would elapse.

Satan was rewarded for his decision to be patient and to trust that God would not play a trick on him—and the little red fellow whispered to himself:

"More people equals fewer resources equals deeper poverty equals greater misery equals more sin equals additional burning bodies." And then he raised his hands up high and curled his fingers in a really corny and typical bad guy sort of way. His eyes lit with the thought of torment, and he spewed saliva while loudly rejoicing the words, "I will have a terrific bonfire!"

Well, since 1811, Satan has been wringing his hands because, being the bright man that he is, he foresaw that wars must slow down relative to birthrates, disease would be reined in through modern medicine, and thus, the population must grow. He figured out as easily as anyone that the more people there are, the more sinners there are. No matter what event may take place on Earth, he reasoned, the cumulative sinner quotient rises as the population rises. "Exponentially, on top of that!" I think is what he said.

Ironically (or fittingly, I'm not sure which), it was God's words, "Be fruitful and multiply," that really made that equation exponential, and Satan's joy all the more.

This brings us to the purpose of this tour, this diversion. It is my task to keep Satan preoccupied beyond the year 2033—Jesus' 2033rd birthday! If I succeed, then Satan has blown his chance to, and I quote, "…be loosed on the earth." Also, we get another thousand years to try to figure out how to ward off Satan's next big shot at Armageddon.

But if I fail, all I can say to you is: if you haven't already, repent.

An Invitation
Nichelle Halseth

I lay you down like emotional entropy
smashing you
pulling you in
first comes the sound
then comes the changing colors that represent the pulsating mass deep down inside you
like infinite regression I want to do it again
Skin
Soft as silk
and thoughts much louder than my voice
you will see what I am made of if you touch me

fast-forward

fast-forward to where I become that secret you keep who has nothing to do with your discipline
it won't happen again
we were two concepts that refined and did not hold true to the undefined
it won't happen

again

It was worship that felt like apprehension when
you told me that the sun exploded over the horizon the moment poetry killed philosophy with a verb—I want you like that continuous push forward

trust and fear at the same time

We speak in tongues to communicate observation
and immerse ourselves in perception
the narcissistic voyeur in me wants to watch
I didn't ask your permission

So if what we write is the future, then
MINE—in big bold letters
between your legs—
would be a ritual
This sacrifice is what I control
So do not underestimate my fury
my sex
my beauty
a painful existence
And as I taste you
you remind me of the sea
salty dark desires you keep

they go deeper

Just like my fingers
Do I make it hard to focus?
Are you suddenly suffering from duality?
How about I chase you down to where your voice
becomes a distraction from insanity
I should have brought an extra pair of panties cuz
Letting you enter where naïveté takes hold
discovering the blind spot was an abstraction
knocking down walls
I create my own diversion
ten medians of the flesh
Countless others I suspect

Eagles
Rick Carl

Eagles are known as messengers to the gods
Carrying our prayers, our hopes, our dreams
Flying the highest and seeing the farthest
King of the birds, by any means

We see them soaring high overhead
When morning first shows its beams
Ruling their kingdom and showing their grace
Near our country's rivers and streams

We chose the bald eagle as our national bird
A bird so regal in flight
When out of war this country emerged
By the dawns so early light

So to the eagle we now give praise
And perform a solemn rite
Upon the eagle we can depend
When morning turns into night

Morning Ritual
Devon Seale

THE SKY WAS JUST GETTING light, the world just starting to wake up. The sun would rise soon. As he did every morning, Dances-Under-Stars walked quietly through the darkened world until he found what he was looking for—a spot with plenty of space, but surrounded by trees and plants. It wasn't too far from the camp. In fact, it was still well within sight, but far enough away to afford him the few moments of privacy he needed. Wearing nothing more than his loincloth, the young Salandran slowly dropped to his knees, bowed his head, and listened.

In the quiet of the early morning, he could hear it. The first beats of the World-Song, a rhythm that only he seemed able to hear. The sounds of the birds as they began to wake, chirping amongst themselves. The first buzzes of insects. The occasional rustle of leaves as the breeze flowed across them. The snap of a twig under an animal's paw. He smiled to himself and listened, his tail beginning to move from side to side, slowly weaving through the grass.

The sound of birds grew. Chirps of different pitch, high and low, fast and slow, soft and harsh. Different patterns formed between the birds as they spoke to welcome the morning. Different sounds all mixing together into a pattern that wasn't a pattern, but still he could hear it. The insects, buzzing near and far, brought an undertone to the chirps, rising and falling with the birds above. The leaves rustled quietly, lending their own percussion to the song that formed. Slowly, his body began to sway, a lithe blue form moving back and forth in the light of the breaking day.

In his mind, he called out to the All-Maker, asking that his offering, his own contribution to the World-Song, be accepted. The World-Song grew. Wind brushed past him, making a small hum in his ear holes. More birds joined in, their chirps and whistles harmonizing with the others. The buzz of insects waxed and waned. And so his body swayed.

The moment the light of the sun finally touched his dark blue skin, making the white spots seem to glow, he leaned forward, his fist touching the ground, one leg moving forward so that he pressed his foot into the grass. A moment later, he spun standing up, and reached out toward the heavens above, the breeze caressing his body. The chirps began their cycle anew, and a bee buzzed past his ear. He turned in one fluid motion as he swept one arm down, then arched it back up, the other arm reaching toward the ground.

Shifting his legs, he stepped forward, then twisted again, spinning, then arching his back, leaning so that his chest was open to the morning sky, his tail swishing behind him. The sound of something knocking on wood echoed through the trees. He swept his upper body around, arching forward to again touch the ground. The knocking came a second time. The whistles above reached a new height, and with them he leaped, spinning through the air, then landed in a crouch, one knee touching the ground.

Again, he reached for the sky, both arms sweeping up, his hips rolling as he stood then slowly turned. His upper body moved first, twisting away from the rising sun. Then his legs moved, stepping in time to the buzz of insects and the rustle of leaves, flowing like liquid through the air as one foot followed the other to arc high into the air, then settle on the ground. Bending, he reached down toward the earth then spread his arms wide as he rose, arching toward the sky above.

And so went his dance, weaving between chirps and whistles, buzzes and rustles. Twigs snapped and wood knocked. He danced on to music few could truly hear. His body flowed, twisting and spinning, sometimes fast and sometimes slow, but always in time to the beat of the World-Song. Ebb and flow, fast and slow, stretch and spin. On and on for minutes on end.

Finally, though the World-Song would never end, Dances-Under-Stars finished his dance, making one last leap into the air, twirling into a final spin, which continued even as he landed on the ground, his feet twisting through the grass before finally he dropped back down to his knees. His arms stretched up once more, then came to settle in his lap as he again bowed his head, his body still swaying to the sounds of the world.

For a long time he swayed and listened. Then he slowly stood, his golden eyes opening for the first time since his dance had begun. A smile still on his lips, he thanked the All-Maker for the beauty of the morning, and for the chance to add his dance to that beauty. He then turned and headed back toward camp, lightly stepping in time with the beat of the World-Song.

Salmon Run
John Sibley Williams

The river comes bloody to our shore and we are thinking
less of causes than how to abstain from drinking.
Hands form a perfect cup, our mouths oval into
a perfect thirst. It is hard

but a good thing to say *no* sometimes
to these choiring fish and violent incisions of sawgrass.
It is good, this struggle. The heavens
and the earth can only keep us

inside so long. Shores erode and all
of a sudden we are chin-deep and vanishing
upstream in bundled schools toward whatever
it was our great-grandfathers were,

toward the temporary holiness of knowing
all my mistakes have been made before.

River, angry

old river, I understand your need to run
swiftly from the source. I too don't look back
at the mountains, so distant, dawn-red,

where I am headed to spawn.

Hailey

Kelly Samarah

It's perfect. The rain washes everything clean.

Hailey crossed her arms. She ignored the thought. It wasn't always easy. Sometimes her thoughts had minds of their own.

"Are the animals in?" Hailey turned from the window to look into her sister's pinched face. Beatie had always hated storms.

"Yes, Beatie. And I made sure to bolt the door." She looked out the window again as Beatie came to stand beside her. "Where's Jonathan?"

"He drove into town. He thinks we'll lose the lights. He insisted we need batteries for the flashlights." Beatie closed the curtains against the gathering wind and rain. "Come. I made us something to eat."

Hailey followed her older sister through the living room, decorated with their deceased parent's old furnishings, and into the warm kitchen. A plate of biscuits and a pot of stew sat on the table. She sat in the chair closest to the stove. Jonathan hated the old stove. He thought they should get an electric one. "More modern," that was his mantra. But Hailey liked the smell of the oven when the fire was lit below. It reminded her of their mother.

Dead, dead, dead. They shouldn't be dead.

"Sshh," Hailey warned the thought.

"Did you say something?" Beatie asked as she set a bowl of stew in front of her.

"No, Beatie," Hailey lied. "I was just reminiscing out loud, I suppose."

"Ah. About what?" Beatie stared hard at her. She didn't like when Hailey spoke of their parents. Hailey closed her lips around a memory.

"Just hoping the storm isn't too terrible."

"That's not reminiscing, my dear. That's worrying." Beatie kept her eyes on Hailey a second longer. Just long enough to make Hailey squirm.

They ate in silence for a few moments. Outside, the wind was picking up. It moaned as it pushed against the sides of the house. Rain pelted the window, long streams of water running down the pane.

Like the house was crying.

"I do hope Jonathan is alright." Hailey looked up at her sister. Beatie brushed a loose strand of ashy blonde hair from her forehead. Hailey had always been envious of her hair and her crystal blue eyes—so light and feminine next to her own dark hair and brown irises.

"He's a big boy. He can handle himself," Beatie made light of Hailey's fears. Always the big sister. She constantly made Hailey feel like a small worrisome child.

They finished their dinner and Hailey stood to clear the dishes. Beatie left the kitchen, and the dishes, to her younger sister. The menial jobs were always left for her. She never complained. It was what it was.

You should complain. It's always the same. Good little Hailey, doing what she's told.

"Quiet, you," Hailey whispered to her thoughts. They never let her alone, filling her head day and night. At times, there seemed to be too many thoughts for her to sift through. Too many different opinions. They always had a comment or a suggestion.

Sometimes, they argued with each other.

Hailey placed the large stew pot in the sink of soapy water. She paused before she began scrubbing and glanced out the window above the sink. It was getting dark, the sun setting behind black clouds. From this side of the house she couldn't see the barn, but she was confident it was fine. She had latched the door tight. Beatie would be pleased.

Hailey focused again on the pot, washing away the leftover stew. She let her thoughts fall over one another, happy to have a distraction. It was always easier to ignore them when her hands were busy.

Beatie never washes dishes... in the family room with her books... yes, sitting in her chair... Mother's chair... you know talking about her is hard... her and Father... makes Hailey sad... sad... so what? She's always sad...Yes, that's true...

"It isn't," Hailey whispered. She wasn't always sad.

Beatie should be stopped.

This was a new thought. It was deep and louder than the rest, resonating over all the others. She didn't like this thought. All her other thoughts went silent when it spoke up.

Stop it! Hailey scrubbed hard at the pot, sloshing water over the edge of the sink and onto her toes. "Stop," she said out loud.

They would *still be here—*

"NO!" Hailey screamed and threw her hands over her ears. The voice stopped abruptly.

"What are you doing in here?" Hailey turned. Beatie stood in the doorway. She held a hardback book in one hand, her finger keeping her place. She looked at Hailey like she was detestable, watching the sudsy water drip from her ears to her shoulders and splatter onto the faded linoleum.

Outside, thunder cracked the sky open and lightening lit the dark evening.

"Nothing. I'm just washing the dishes," she said quietly. She turned back to the sink, but she could still feel Beatie's eyes boring into her. The hairs on her neck prickled and stood rigid. When Hailey finally dared to glance over her shoulder again, Beatie was gone. She sighed, relieved, then lifted the pot from the water and began to dry it.

It wouldn't be hard... Hailey's hands slowed their circular motion. The voice hadn't left. It had only gone quiet for a moment.

Feel the weight of it. Heavy enough to break something...

Hailey set the pot on the counter and stared at it.

Good little Hailey. She's always very careful.

Hailey wanted her other thoughts back. This lone voice made her head ache. She rubbed her temples, and spoke loudly inside her head. *LEAVE me ALONE!* She placed the bowls and silverware in the water and began washing vigorously. She searched her head for the familiar drone of thoughts she had grown accustom to, but they were gone. The silence was unnerving, an eerie background to the one persistent voice that remained.

She doesn't care about you or anyone else. She only cares about herself. You know it's true, you're just too weak to do anything about it.

"I said leave me alone!" Hailey clamped her lips together and looked over her shoulder. She waited for Beatie to reappear. When she didn't, Hailey blew a loose strand of hair away from her eyes and turned back to the sink.

I love my sister. She takes care of me, and all the important things. The farm would have gone to the bank if not for Beatie. If the voice wasn't to be ignored, Hailey was going to set it straight.

You're such a blind, stupid girl. And a coward.

Hailey set a bowl in the adjacent sink a little too harshly. It clattered, and a chip flew from the side and pinged off the porcelain basin.

Hailey stared at it. *Now look what you made me do! I chipped the bowl! Beatie will be furious!* She quickly picked up the chipped piece and threw it in the garbage can. *Maybe she won't notice. If I hide the bowl in the back of the cupboard...*

Listen to yourself! Getting all in a frenzy over a broken dish! Why? Because Beatie will be angry!

Of course it's because she will be angry! I don't like when she is angry with me. Hailey took a deep breath. *And I'm not a coward.*

Oh yes, you are. A yellow ninny.

Just leave me alone! Hailey slapped her forehead with three quick, sharp taps. When she lowered her hand, the voice was quiet. She smiled to herself and quickly finished the dishes.

Beatie was lounging in the recliner when she entered the living room. A fire crackled behind the black door of their potbellied wood stove. The lamp on the table next to her sister lit up the room with soft, yellow light.

"Did you finish the dishes?" Beatie looked up from her book.

"Yes, Beatie, all done."

"Good girl. Now, go fetch some firewood before the storm gets too bad." Beatie returned to her book.

Hailey mumbled a compliance, grabbed her coat from the hook on the wall, and headed for the front door. She slipped it on and turned to her sister. Beatie sat like royalty, her neck and shoulders straight, her chin tilted just slightly. Even the way she licked her finger and turned the page seemed majestic.

Hailey suppressed a smile as she said, "Beatie, you have some dinner on your dress."

Beatie's head snapped up, and she glared at Hailey. "Thank you, Hailey," She said slowly and curtly. "The firewood?"

Hailey nodded, looking at the small brown stain on the front of Beatie's dress. It was dry, but Beatie wiped at it, hard.

Hailey closed the door on her irritated sister. The wind and rain beat down on her as she stepped from the porch. It was fully dark now. She quietly chastised herself for not bringing a flashlight, but didn't want to face Beatie's stare that would accuse her of being slow-witted were she to go back in.

The woodshed was set far behind their old, three story farmhouse and nestled underneath two towering oak trees. Their branches waved to her as she pushed her way through the wind. Rain was already penetrating her coat as she squeezed into the small space inside the door.

I should check on the animals. She could hear their milk cow, Bonnie, moo woefully from the barn.

So worried about the animals... what about Jonathan?

Hailey began stacking wood in her arms.

He should've been back by now.

"Jonathan will come home when he's done. He's probably just waiting out the storm." She hadn't meant to answer. She didn't want to validate any of the voice's assumptions.

They've been arguing lately...

"They always argue."

You know it's gotten worse.

"So what? Families have arguments. It's stressful running the farm."

That's not the only reason.

Hailey shook her head. She wasn't going to think about it. She hated when her siblings fought. The way Beatie glared at Jonathan when he wasn't looking scared her. Beatie was the oldest, but Jonathan was the man of the house, now that Father was gone. Just last week, Hailey had sat at the top of the stairs listening as they exchanged heated words in the kitchen below.

"You're going to drive this place into the ground!" Jonathan had yelled.

A single thud—his fist on the table.

"That's not your concern. I'm calling the shots here. I'm listed first in the will." Beatie's calm voice was a taunt to Jonathan's anger.

"You think that's going to matter when we're homeless?"

"That won't happen."

"You're so sure of yourself, you naive bitch. We need something to show for the cost of running this place! The insurance money is gone—"

"No thanks to you." Beatie spit back at him heatedly.

"It was split equally! Where's your money? And Hailey's? You spent twice as much as me. On what? An old milk cow and seed we never used!"

"And what about you? You spent all of your money on that shiny piece of glorified steel! A truck that's as useless as you are!"

A slap, skin connecting with skin.

Beatie gasped and Hailey cringed, hiding her face in her hands.

"Don't you ever touch me again, you bastard! I'll have the sheriff arrest you faster than you can jump in your whore wagon." Beatie's footsteps grew louder as she left the kitchen. She was at the bottom of the stairs with Jonathan on her heels. He grabbed her arm and spun her around. Hailey scooted back into the shadows, unseen.

"I won't let you do this to us. I'll stop you." Jonathan was inches from Beatie's face.

"Oh, dear brother." Beatie leaned an inch closer and kissed him on the tip of his nose. "Not if I stop you first."

Jonathan pushed her away with a sickened grunt and wiped his arm across his nose. Beatie laughed as he walked out and slammed the front door.

Hailey stood motionless, staring at the wood in her hand, as she remembered the tension between her siblings.

Jonathan was standing in her way. So she got rid of him. How long before she gets rid of you, too?

"She wouldn't do that," she whispered.

Wake up! Beatie would do anything to keep her life the way she wants it. What about your parents? They were—

"No! I told you I didn't want to talk about that! Beatie is our sister. She loves us. She wouldn't do anything to hurt me or Jonathan."

Wouldn't she?

"Enough!" she yelled. She backed out of the shed with her armful of wood and went back to the house.

"Beatie, I got the wood..." Her voice lost sound when she came through the door. Beatie wasn't in the chair. "Beatie?" she called. She dropped the wood in the box by the stove.

She checked the bathroom, but the door was open and the light was off. *She must have gone to change her dress.* Hailey went to the stairs and called up, "Beatie?" No answer. She climbed three steps and called again. "Beatie?"

She knows you're onto her.

"Don't be ridiculous. I'm not onto anything." She climbed the stairs slowly. Outside, thunder crashed. Suddenly, there was a pop and the house went dark. Hailey sucked in her breath and leaned against the wall, holding her chest. When her eyes had adjusted to the unexpected darkness, she crept up to Beatie's bedroom door. It was open a crack, and she pushed it the rest of the way. The dry hinges croaked.

"Beatie, are you in here?" Hailey could hardly see in the unlit room, until lightening lit the world outside again and poured through the window. For a second, Hailey saw the bed, the tidy dresser, and all corners of the room. Beatie wasn't there. She turned and headed back downstairs.

She's hiding! Waiting to pounce on you when you least expect it. You have to stop her. You have to! Before she does to you what she did to Jonathan! Before she sends you where she sent your parents!

"She wouldn't… she can't… sh-she loves me." Hailey was confused. Where *was* Beatie? Why wasn't she answering? She went to the kitchen. On the counter was the pot from dinner.

…heavy enough to cause some damage.

"No," Hailey shook her head.

You have to kill her before she kills you.

"Never!" But Hailey found herself stepping toward the heavy black kettle.

Think of what she's done already. If not for yourself, do it for Mother and Father.

"I can't," she said, even as her hand was wrapping itself around the curved handle.

You can. You don't have to let her push you around.

The pot hung from her hand like a boulder as she trudged out of the kitchen and to the front door. She set it at her feet and swung the door open. Without the porch light, darkness swallowed everything. Thunder grumbled above her, urging her forward.

Hailey's feet knew their way to the barn. When she reached it, a loud bang made her jump then go still, until lightening lit up the face of the barn and she saw that the door had been unbolted. The wind pulled it forward again, then slammed it shut with another boom.

Hailey went inside and to the right where flashlights hung on the wall. She set the kettle down and shook out her hand before grabbing one and clicking it on.

Careful. If she's in here, you don't want her to catch you by surprise.

"Beatie?" Hailey called. She picked the pot up with her free hand and swung the flashlight beam around. "Beeaatiee?" She shone the light toward the stalls and on the face of Bonnie, who mooed at her with wild eyes. She flung the flashlight to the right and their goat, Blackie, bleated pitifully.

The barn shook.

She's not here, Hailey told the voice.

She has to be here somewhere. She has no car, and the storm… she can't be far.

"But where is she?" Hailey went back to the door, but before she could step out into the turbulent night, something gripped her shoulder from behind. Hailey dropped the kettle and whirled around, grappling with the flashlight. It shot its beam at the ceiling, then to the side, before her fumbling hands righted it and her brother's face was revealed.

"Jonathan!" He put one hand up and squinted at her.

"Get that damn light out of my face, Hailey!"

"Jonathan, you're home! We were worried…" A wave of guilt washed over her. How could she have thought such horrible things about Beatie? She blamed the voice. "Um, is Beatie out here with you?" She swallowed, but her dry throat refused to be moistened.

"Uh… no," Jonathan cleared his own throat. "Isn't she inside?" Jonathan pushed past her to the door.

"No, no she's not," Hailey said quickly.

"Well, she's not out here." Jonathan opened the door with Hailey on his heels. As an afterthought, she went back and grabbed the pot.

Jonathan fought with the wind to get the door closed. He bolted it tight and turned to Hailey. "What're you doing with that pot?"

Hailey looked at the kettle in her hand. She opened her mouth, but no words would come. She couldn't tell him the truth.

The voice whispered behind her ears. *Lie.*

Hailey stuttered. "I-I was just… I was going to use it."

"We have buckets. You don't need to use our pot for anything in the barn." He reached for it, but Hailey pulled it back.

"I have it. I'll take it back in."

She heard him sigh. "I have to get something from my truck. You go inside."

"But Beatie—"

"Don't worry about Beatie! Do as I say!" Jonathan yelled, and Hailey cowered away from him. He went past her to the side of the barn.

This was stupid. I should've never listened to you! Do you know what I almost did? When the voice didn't answer, she grew angrier. *I'm not listening to you anymore!*

Finally, it spoke. *What was Jonathan doing in the barn?*

He can go in the barn if he wants to. There's no law says he can't. Yet, the question made her pause. She was almost to the house when she looked back at the barn. Turning quickly, she headed back the way she'd come.

I'm going to show you. He's just getting something from his truck, that's all. And Beatie probably went for a walk…

In this weather? She's terrified of thunderstorms.

Shut up. You're making me think things that aren't true.

The barn door was still bolted shut. She gripped the handle of the pot tight and went around the side. There were fresh tire tracks in the deep mud beside the barn. They went all the way around to the back of the building. Hailey followed them, wondering why Jonathan hadn't parked closer to the house.

When she got behind the barn, Hailey raised her flashlight. There was Jonathan's truck, but she didn't see her brother. She thought about calling out to him, but the voice piped up. *No, wait.*

Hailey put her hand over the lens of the flashlight and doused its glow. She peered into the darkness and listened, but the storm overrode all her senses. She stepped closer to the truck. Lightening flashed, brightening the dark night briefly. Hailey spotted her brother near the front of the truck.

She aimed the flashlight at him. Jonathan was hunched over a muddy bulk. The rain had turned his blonde hair murky brown and laid it sleek and smooth against his head. The water soaked through his shirt, transforming the color from gray to smoky black, but not washing away the dark red splotches that covered the front. He straightened, slowly, and stepped toward Hailey.

"Jonathan!" she screamed. "What've you done?!"

"Hailey, listen to me!"

"Jonathan, no!" She flung the beam toward the ground. Beatie's lifeless face, covered in red mud, stared up at her.

"Hailey, it had to be done! She would've ruined us!" He stepped toward her again. "Did you want to live under her thumb forever?" The words caused her to whip her head back to her brother. Those words... something about those words...

Think, Hailey. Think hard. The voice was louder now, forcing her to remember.

Beatie in the kitchen. Two trays. Two bowls of soup. A bottle of yellow liquid. The smell burned Hailey's nose when Beatie removed the cap. The funeral. Beatie gripping her hand too tight, leading her off to the side where no one could hear. "... had to be done, Hailey. Did you want to live under their thumbs forever?"

Hailey's teeth clamped together, catching her tongue and sending the metal flavor of her blood down her throat. She looked at her brother, at his eyes too wide in his head and his chest that rose and fell with his heavy breaths.

He's no better, Hailey.

"Hailey?" Jonathan reached his hand toward her. Hailey backed up.

"Don't touch me!"

Jonathan charged her. Hailey lifted the pot and swung. It connected with the side of Jonathan's face and sent him flying into the side of the truck. She dropped the flashlight and used both hands to lift it above her head and bring it down on Jonathan's smooth, wet hair. She hammered the pot into his skull until his arms stopped twitching in the glow of the flashlight lying in the mud.

Hailey fell to her knees. She let the pot fall from her hands.

Everything is as it should be now, Hailey. Everything is right. Hailey looked at the bodies of her brother and sister.

Now you call the shots, Hailey.

"Now I call the shots."

No more thumbs to live under.

"No more thumbs," Hailey murmured. "I call the shots."

That's right. You and I. Now, be a good girl and go find a shovel.

She stood on shaky legs and followed the tracks back to the front of the barn.

That's a good girl, the voice cooed.

Hailey smiled.

Her, Not Her
Nichelle Halseth

Disassembling you to replace pieces that lock into me
I touch your stomach, my left hand around your neck
One leg over my shoulder
I feel the matter of where a star used to be
no names
just teeth
I contract, ready for eruptions coming after I see your eyes on my mouth
my mouth on everything you've got
everything you've got inside of me
where I listen like the two of cups combining
they'll not be able to tell us apart
and intertwined, our bodies recite our dialogue in tantra
You
are like a supernova intricately tracing your veins with my blood
They are everywhere you have been
Man is not designed to survive this
a death wish
I breathe it like your scent
like the time I got up early
Is this my punishment for wanting you to look at me?
I want to taste it in the sweat from the heat you kept in your chest
and sketching the galaxies of someone else's solar system on your back with my
fingernails
like ammunition
it becomes self-fixing
when you walk into a room unconscious conditioning gives
nervous tension dialogue for specific intentions

Struck by beauty!

No safe words, just undertones and a fuck you
No line breaks, just raw consciousness

I'm reveling in the wait
it's like foreplay… tease, tease, tease me into oblivion so this growling
in my soul can cease
it's not abuse cuz I know you're into this
Feed me more than a taste of those disassembled pieces
I want them ripped apart and nailed to my wall
so that when the blood trickles down I can call it whatever I want
But I won't call it art
This unfinished masterpiece will bare the body nude, adorned only
with the paint strokes and Sharpie love notes you placed upon me
but
You didn't promise me shit
so I start creeping up your esophagus like ivy before sunrise
ready to choke the objective from a very dangerous game
and you scream equations of relation to my pupils as they dilate and
you decide that I need MORE
but
you did not promise me shit
and you will not win

Seasons Of The Wild

Jacqueline Carl

(An Excerpt)

"Go ahead," Morgan told them. "Make a wish." She took the ornament out of its box, looked toward the sky, and spoke her own wish out loud. "I wish I knew why someone wants this thing so badly."

"It's been quiet," said Lucan. "Maybe whoever wants it has given up by now."

"Maybe, but not likely," said Morgan. "They've gone through an awful lot of trouble for it so far."

"Aaaahhhh." Lawren screamed as large black wings beat down on her back. Cyrano, tether trailing behind, appeared from nowhere. His giant wings knocked Lawren's glasses off as the determined buzzard tried to push past her to get to Morgan… no, to get to the Christmas tree topper, which glittered in the sunlight like a giant jewel.

Lawren bumped into Morgan trying to escape the bird, nearly knocking her to the ground. Lucan caught her before she fell, but not before Morgan dropped the crystal star.

Cyrano landed between them, folded his wings, and looked up innocently before turning his attention back to his prize. He started to peck at the glass, greedily shoving it around on the ground.

Morgan righted herself. She could feel her face flush as she pushed away from Lucan. She scolded the errant vulture. "Not again, you little monster. How did you get away this time?" She looked around for the volunteer who should be watching him, but that person either hadn't missed the bird yet, or hadn't caught up with him.

Morgan stepped on Cyrano's leash to trap him, hoping her jeans and tennis shoes would protect her from the bird's strong beak. But Cyrano wasn't thinking about escape, concentrating instead on the bright red heart in the center of the ornament. *Probably attracted to the color*, thought Morgan. *Or the glitter.*

"He can't break anything, can he?" asked Lucan.

"I don't think so," said Morgan. "It's pretty solid."

"He sure loves sparkly things, doesn't he?" Lawren laughed, having recovered her glasses and her composure.

Morgan bent over to pick up the ornament before the vulture actually managed to break it. Before she could take it from him, the heart snapped open. A small leather pouch, folded over and tied with a thin leather strap, was stuffed inside.

"What's that?" Lawren took a step closer, forgetting about the vulture's mock attack.

"I'm not sure." Morgan pulled at the stiff ties. The pouch itself was soft and opened easily. She tipped the contents into her hand and gasped. Two rings slid out. One looked hand-carved. Dark and light woods polished to a smooth finish floated side-by-side changing positions once, like a Mobius. Morgan could see the details of each tree inside the wood. It felt alive. The second ring was also to die for—a gold band that twisted once, with a channel of small diamonds. An inscription etched in the metal read *For Eternity*. "They look like wedding bands," she said.

The rings tingled warmly in her hand. For one brief moment, Morgan felt like she was sleep walking, out of step with time, as the rings told their story—one of lovers whose feelings began as soft and fragile as wood, then grew into an enduring romance. Lucan's hand on Morgan's shoulder yanked her back to the here and now. She teetered, unsteady.

"You okay?" Blue eyes searched hers. "You disappeared on us for a minute."

Morgan nodded. Her attention was pulled to the ground as Cyrano bobbed up and down, begging for the return of his prize.

"Oh, thank goodness." Sonny was huffing by the time she caught up with the vulture. The volunteer pushed back a strand of hair that had escaped her waist-length gray braid. She tucked her tie-dyed tee shirt back into her oversized overalls as best as her gloved hands would allow. "I thought he was gone for sure this time."

Morgan palmed the rings and hid them behind her back. She heaved a sigh, glad Sonny had come to collect the vulture before he stopped begging for his loot and started demanding it.

"Come here, you little hooligan." The elderly volunteer scooped up the eight-pound bird, snagging the tether before he could take off again. She nodded at the open star. "Oh! I hope he hasn't broken your decoration." She admonished the vulture before heading up the Nature Trail to Cyrano's mews. "You've been a naughty boy."

Lucan picked up the ornament and snapped it together. The internal hinge and joint closed seamlessly. "What a break. We might never have found that secret compartment."

Crows
Rick Carl

Crows are keepers of the sacred law
For nothing escapes their sight
They're our guides to the spirit world
And keep us from our plight

They'll light your way, and guide your hand
When your day seems dark as night
If you follow their path, straight and true,
They'll lead you into the light

They bring a message of magical change
And give us a choice that's right
When you meet a crow in the path of life
You'll have a future bright

Unfinished business is their milieu
Though it's not so black and white
All magic comes with a price
So don't choose the dark over light

But best beware and travel with care
Because crows are tricksters too
It can't be helped, it is their way,
They may play a trick on you

Crows are clever, crows are wise,
Crows love a good joke or two
Crows might wait their entire lives
To play that joke on you

So seek their guidance, consider their word,
But follow a path that's true
Their wisdom and knowledge can be your guide
In everything that you do

Useful Equipment
Esther Wood
(An Excerpt)

Zume discovers her new world.

Zume didn't know why Narg said she'd get to choose her clothes. There weren't any in the closet. Just bikini tops and bottoms in a variety of colors and styles. The little bug-like guy urged her to wear something that wasn't much more than strategically placed chains. "This would please Culantor most," he said.

"I don't care what he wants, whoever he is!" she said, ignoring his protests. "I'm not going to parade around in hardware and pretend I'm dressed." Crossing her arms was all but impossible with the masses of flesh between them. She grabbed the chains and threw them to the white tile floor. It was satisfying to see Narg shrink away, even though she didn't have the strength to make much of a noise with them.

"Wear what you will, then." His voice cracked midsentence.

She picked out a pink polka-dotted top and a bottom with orange stripes because they were the two pieces that contained the most cloth. That wasn't saying much. The bottom just barely covered Zume's butt cheeks and the top revealed far more cleavage than Power Girl's outfit did. She discovered she wouldn't need to shave her legs or armpits, because her body was as smooth as a baby from the eyes down.

Narg didn't give Zume the courtesy of privacy. But he didn't seem lecherous either. He watched her with about the same regard as her drill sergeant had watching her clean a gun. Once she was ready, he pressed the wall and the closet snapped shut. He pressed the wall again and an open doorway appeared. He took her hand and pulled her through. "Come along."

The door disappeared as soon as Zume entered the hallway. She blinked. A white luminous tube completely surrounded her and Narg. The floor looked as smooth and firm as the walls and ceiling, but felt soft and warm under Zume's bare feet. There were no doors or windows. No escape.

Zume saw no reference points to gauge the distance; she didn't know how far they'd walked by the time the hallway suddenly widened into a large room. A series of long, dark-red curtains divided each side of the room into three sections, and the aisle between them was more than wide enough to drive a Hummer down to the large desk at the other end. Tightening his grip on her hand, Narg stopped in front of the first set of curtain panels. "Look down and wait."

"Yeah right," she muttered. Like she was going to just stand there and do that. No way. Not when there was so much about this place she didn't know yet.

The curtain panels seemed to be made of thick velvet and were so long that the fabric puddled on the floor. Lights played with the shadows on the closest ones in such a way that Zume felt like she was standing in front of two bloody waterfalls. She couldn't see what supported them; it was like they poured down from dark clouds instead of a ceiling.

The room teemed with turtle-guys, all dressed in identical white tunics. One hovered near the middle section on the right side of the aisle, bearing an empty tray. Two of them stood in front of the desk, talking with a huge beefy man with gray skin. Another emerged from the shadows behind Narg, carrying a tray laden with food and drinks. The little bug-guy nudged Zume to the side, allowing her a glimpse into the first section on the left.

Another Barbie doll woman was sitting there, even more naked than Zume, with long, wavy blond hair dipped over one eye. She sat at a metallic table looking at her folded hands that rested on the shiny surface. Without even trying, the woman reeked of sexuality. She looked like that pole dancer Zume and Harold had seen in one of the off-base bars back in their army days. They'd spent the night laughing at the woman's display, because it was so obvious she didn't care one lick about any of the guys vying for her attention.

Zume wasn't laughing now. She tried to recall what her Strategic Procedures instructor had said in case of capture. Keep calm. That was the one thing he stressed most. You'll never be able to see past your nose if you don't stay calm. Study your surroundings. Find your best escape route.

Since the shadows behind her and Narg revealed nothing helpful, Zume turned her attention toward the main desk. The wide gray man sitting behind it had to be the guy in charge. She noticed one of the turtle guys standing in front of him held the hand of a movie-star-handsome guy who wore nothing but a shiny thong. Glancing beyond them, the hulking man put his hands on his desk and stood up. He said something to the other turtle guy, who turned around, dropped his jaw, and headed toward Zume.

Gasping, Narg yanked her arm. "Do not look directly at the Boss!"

"Whatever." Their Boss must have some kind of power issues. "I'd rather watch the good looking guy in front of him, anyway." Ignoring another gasp, she studied the area beyond the desk. So far, she couldn't see anything but shadows there.

Heaving a sigh of relief when the turtle guy reached them, Narg shoved Zume's hand into his. "Willet," said the little bug, "the anomalies in this XK are much worse than we first thought."

Pursing the lumpiness that served as his lips, Willet shook his head. "The Boss is hoping they will smooth out once the bond is made."

"We can only hope this is so." Narg stepped back into the shadows behind them and disappeared.

Even though she towered over him, Willet pulled Zume's hand and drew her along as if she was a little kid. So she dragged her heels like a stubborn three-year-old. That gave her the chance to study the sections between the curtains. The one on her right held a shiny silver table and four empty chairs. No doors or windows. The Barbie with the long wavy hair occupied the one on the other side of Willet. She wore the chains Narg had favored. Next to her, a pixie-like person with a big plume of lavender hair sat at the far wall. The pixie caught Zume looking into their booth and turned to speak to someone across the table from the Barbie.

Willet jerked her away. "You must avoid all eye contact until you meet Culantor."

"Who's Culantor?"

"Just look down."

She turned her gaze toward the desk, where a tall burly woman took the handsome man from the turtle guy in front of the desk and headed for one of the closer booths. The woman was as gray-skinned as the Boss and far more muscular than Zume had been before she got turned into a Barbie. "Geez, why didn't you make me look like her?"

"What?" Willet's scaly forehead furrowed. "Can it be you see that woman?"

Zume frowned. "Well, of course I can. She's only a few yards away from us."

"Oh, this is bad," he muttered. "An XK pet should not be able to see her master's spouse or the YK pet."

"Why?" All Zume's blood dropped to her feet. She suspected she was in a very bad place. "Is this a b-brothel?"

"Brothel?" Willet looked confused. Then his language program must have kicked in, because his face lit with understanding. "No, that would be in the Rental Sector. This is where the Boss introduces his clients to their pet sex slaves."

"What?! No way!" She yanked her hand free and bolted back toward the entrance. The door had to be there somewhere.

She ran smack into a man wearing a hat and black trench coat that made him look like Indiana Jones meets The Matrix. "Easy does it." He grabbed her arm and held her as Willet caught up with them. "I'll help you," he said, but Zume couldn't tell whether he was speaking to her or the turtle-guy.

Willet eyed the skinny guy in the trench coat. "I need to get this one bonded immediately."

Trench coat nodded. "I can see that. However, I have pressing business with Tutalin." He pointed behind him where the pixie was towing the other Barbie by the hand, her fancy chains jingling in rhythm with her steps. "I'm sure you wouldn't want to make him wait for his recovered property."

"No, Fletcher." Willet sounded as resigned as Zume felt. "Go ahead."

Touching the rim of his hat, Fletcher said, "This won't take long." Zume noticed he was several inches shorter than the Barbie-woman he took from his pixie friend. Ushering her to the vacant side of the Boss's desk as if he owned the place, he ordered the Barbie-woman to look down and turned his gaze on the massive gray man. "Mission accomplished, Tutalin."

The Boss—Tutalin—gave him a satisfied grin. "Well done, Fletcher. How's my girl?"

"Medical says she's no worse for wear and tear."

Tutalin nodded thoughtfully. "Good. And the perpetrator? Will he suit your purposes?"

Fletcher shrugged. "He's as big and strong as Culantor there—" he jerked his head toward the beefy man on the other side of Tutalin—"but he's stupid. I suppose I could invest in a few programs to make him smarter, but that'd put me further into debt than I was hoping to go."

"Your credit is good here. If that's what you want, we'll make it happen."

"I'll think about it. In the meantime, he's in the holding tank."

Tutalin chuckled. "If that man doesn't suit you, I'll give you credits for him. I have a pressing need for slaves in the palladium mines." He turned to the big man standing nearby. "Take this as a warning, Culantor. If you try to steal my slaves, you will pay for it with your life."

The wide gray man-Culantor-ran a hand over his slick black hair. A muscle in his large jaw twitched. "What are you talking about, Tutalin? We have paid a good part of our debt already."

Tutalin nodded. "So you have; and I expect you and Latulu will treat your new slaves with care."

Willet nudged Zume forward. "Look into your new owner's eyes and you will fall in love with him."

Culantor's smile revealed canines as long as a dog's. "Let's see if you're worth the credits I paid," he said in a husky voice.

She dropped her eyes to his thick gray neck. The deep V-cut in his shirt revealed bulging pecs. As he reached for her, his fingers brushed her closest boob, sending a thrill down to her lower regions. Her body responses terrified her. She refused to lose control. "You keep your fat hands off me!"

"Oh, she's a feisty one!"

"I'll show you feisty!" Bunching her fists, she flailed at him. She had to swing wide to get around the extra flesh on her chest. But her arms no longer had power. Her punches did nothing but bounce off his body. She managed to escape the toothy hulk's grasp, but she didn't get to run far.

"That's enough," said a man's voice. His tone was calm. He touched the back of her neck and gently squeezed the cords. Every bit of fear and tension drained away, making her feel limp and compliant. She looked at the floor. The man's long coat dusted his black boots.

The Boss was on his feet. "Thanks, Fletcher."

"What a useless sex pet!" Culantor took steps toward Tutalin. "I demand a refund!"

"Now, let's not get hasty," said the Boss. "I'm sure we can work something out."

"That girl I retrieved is already primed for a new owner," said the man behind Zume.

"Good idea, Fletcher." Tutalin sounded relieved. "How would you like to try her, Culantor?"

Zume ventured a look at the other Barbie. The big-boobed blonde began to smile like she was getting Christmas early this year. Evidently she was eager for Culantor's affections, because as soon as he said he'd try, she ran into his arms, giggling like a stupid bimbo.

"I'll take that as a yes," said Tutalin. "Willet, show them to their table." After they left, he sighed. "I don't know what to do with this one, though. She's over-ridden most of the programs we've installed in her. I guess we'll have to wipe out her intelligence and start over."

"That won't be necessary. I'll take her."

"What? I thought you wanted a bodyguard!"

"I think she's closer to what I need than that idiot I have in holding. How about a trade straight across?"

Tutalin shrugged. "It'd be cheaper for me to turn him into a miner than her into a worthwhile sex pet… " he thought a moment. "It's a deal. We'll talk later, after you've assessed the modifications you'll need."

Fletcher turned Zume around so she was facing him. "You have the choice of being a sex slave or my bodyguard."

She looked down at the battered rim shading his eyes. "I'd rather die than be anyone's s-sex slave."

"Then look at me." Fletcher flicked back his hat and looked up into her face.

Zume noted he was pleasant enough to look at, though he had olive skin—not a Mediterranean tan, but more the color of green olives—with a bow-shaped mouth and a straight nose. His generous yellow eyes, slanted catlike, pierced her soul. All her doubts melted away, as if she'd taken a tranquilizer and the effects had just set in. A feeling of trust washed over her. She felt as if she'd known Fletcher all her life. But, somewhere deep inside, where no one could ever touch her, a tiny voice said, "No!"

When Will Your *Real* Life Begin
Sandra Rokoff-Lizut

when you find the *right* man/woman
ditch the one you have
gain a child or two
see them off to school
or get them out of rehab

when you have the *right* job
the raise, better boss
make more money
show them *what you're made of*

when you write the book
paint the picture
get the degree
finally leave *this crappy job*

when your mother gets better
father dies, father gets better
mother dies—when you've dealt
with the deaths of your parents

when you find the *best* house
town, nation, world
a place that's well run
where everything *works*

when wars are over
the world is kinder
or maybe when you
become a little bit older
older
       older
              older
                     old—

Deadly Deals
Dani Clifton

Rush hour was well underway by the time I reached the Diablo, and already the club was packed. Conversations competed with one another, punctuated by an occasional raised voice and growl. Stale beer, the sweet stench of burning herb alongside that of fine cigars, and something feral just below the surface of it all welcomed me back.

Gus was perched on his three-legged throne just inside the front door. I'd never held Gus's heritage against him; as daemons go, he was an okay guy. Of course, I'd never thought of him as the bent-on-world-domination, baby-eating sort. Being one of the unaligned, Gus owed fealty to no one, neither the Dark nor the Light side of Fae; like everything else in this world or the next, Gus was neither good nor evil—he simply was. He lived a low-key life right here in Portland, the City of Roses, running security for Roane at the club. Though he was personable enough, I had a permanent mental memo to never get on the bouncer's bad side. He was still a daemon, every 6-foot, 3-inch, pitch-black badass ounce of him.

"Bossman's in a mood Isa, best watch yourself." Gus's gravelly voice was low and coarse, as if he were talking around a mouthful of bones.

"Yeah, I know," I nodded guiltily, "who do you think put him there?" Knowing firsthand how volatile Roane's temper could be, I added, "Sorry about that."

"Ain't nothing I can't handle."

With a deep sigh, I moved on toward the bar. Roane caught my eye as soon as I made my way past the pool tables. To avoid confrontation, he turned the stereo up and shot me a stern look. I returned the gesture with a facetious grin, pointed to the sign above the door that read "HAPPY HOUR," and turned my back before he brought our exchange to a full-blown pissing match.

Moody Skinwalkers could be such a pain in my Sídhe ass.

Of course, now I understood why the ubiquitous "they" advise against mixing business with pleasure or sleeping with your boss. Hindsight and all aside, I'd made my bed and had to lie in it. There wasn't much I could do about my poor choices at the moment, so I began my shift by pouring drams of whisky for those seeking solace at the bottom of a bottle. As the only Fae gentleman's club in the city, the Diablo catered to a white-collar crowd. Comfortably assimilated into the human world, the room was full of lawmakers, doctors, and bankers, none of the mortal persuasion.

The Diablo's clientele wouldn't change significantly until the sun went down, when those who were more comfortable sliding among the shadows came out of hiding. What the Diablo served during those hours ran a little more on the macabre side.

After an hour of listening to Carl Orff's Carmina Burana, Roane brought the intensity down a notch by changing the music to something a little mellower; those who were still nursing their drinks took a collective sigh.

"Isa," he beckoned to me in a fresh, civil tone that told me he was about to ask for a favor. "I've got a shipment coming in tonight from a perspective supplier. Gus will be riding shotgun with me out back, so I'll need you to close up on your own."

"No big deal," I answered, keeping my lingering attitude toward him from my voice. No way was I going to give him that sort of satisfaction. "Besides, it'll probably be dead by then." Retrospectively, I really wish I hadn't chosen those exact words.

"Great," Roane's lopsided smile made his cheek dimple, and his green eyes glinted mischievously, making parts of my body tingle. "I owe you one."

His kiss on my cheek was disappointingly chaste, and I scolded myself for noticing the difference. "You owe me much more than that," I countered in a steady voice, but he'd already moved on to something else. I doubted he heard a word I'd said. Or he'd chosen to ignore the truth.

Ours hadn't always been a volatile relationship. In the beginning, all I got to see was the side I wanted to see—the compassionate, loving Roane. It wasn't until I tried to leave and go back home that the alpha of his beast began challenging for control. I loved the man he was, but feared what he could become.

Once upon a time, in the not-so-distant past, Roane had surprised me with a small velvet box, the perfect size to house an engagement ring, which is exactly what I had thought it was. It wasn't a ring; it was a necklace with a .45 caliber, pure silver bullet wrapped in wire and suspended from a silver chain. Pure silver is the only substance that can incapacitate a Skinwalker. In lieu of a ring and a commitment, Roane had presented to me the ways and means to subdue his beast. An escape. A way out that I'd never taken off since that day.

There was no sense dwelling on a past I couldn't change or a future I had little control over, so to distract myself from my commiserating, I began lifting clean glasses from the dishwasher and putting them up on the rack to dry. To keep busy, I transferred another case of Heineken to the cooler, served the crowd as it slowly waned, and made a list of liquors that needed to be restocked, all the while trying to resist the forbidden roads that my mind wanted to travel down. I pushed away the thoughts, but akin to ignoring an irritating tickle at the back of your throat, the more I tried to suppress them, the more they took hold. I'd always known Roane ran in some perilous circles, including The Jesuit's, a fallen angel turned mob boss who imported people from third world countries where humans were far less tainted by pollution, making their flesh more palatable and, in turn, more profitable.

Even worse than contemplating Roane's darker side was contemplating my own, and I didn't want to tackle those demons—of which I had plenty—right at the moment. It'd been centuries since I'd seen my ancestral home, and the way things were working out lately, I wasn't going to be allowed back anytime soon.

The night dragged on. No matter how many glances I threw at the big clock over the door, it still didn't read closing time. The crowd had thinned significantly and the shades that would normally fill the empty seats at dusk were oddly absent. Like any establishment, the Diablo had its slow nights, but this night seemed especially sluggish—eerily so.

The last customer left at half past one and, except for the music still streaming from the speakers, an unusual quiet fell over the place.

At a quarter to two, I watched Gus escort two men upstairs to Roane's office. Five minutes later, Roane joined them from the stockroom in the basement. Their meeting didn't take long; it was only a matter of minutes before Gus, Roane, and their guests, one of whom was carrying an aluminum briefcase, descended the stairs and exited silently through the backdoor that led to the alley behind the club.

As the only employee inside the empty club, I made the executive decision to close down for the night. As I crossed the vacant floor to throw the latch on the front door, a prickling wave of violent energy washed over me. Suddenly, the door crashed open and six intruders charged in, violent energy embodied.

Running on adrenaline-laced reflexes, I turned and sprinted back toward the bar. There was no time to make a plan; I gauged about the place where I knew Roane kept a 9mm Glock—locked and loaded with silver bullets dipped in holy water and dead man's ashes—and dove over the bar. Landing on my feet with cat-like grace, I grabbed the Glock and flicked off the safety with my thumb.

Instinct and self-preservation, the rules of the game were simple: kill, or be killed. In one fluid motion I stood, leveled the gun barrel at the first intruder coming at me, and shot him point-blank. Bits of him sprayed across the counter. The second one was almost on me; I dropped him before even taking another breath. They may or may not have been armed—I didn't take the time to inventory. My bad. The next three that rushed me all dealt themselves loosing hands and a third eye in the center of their foreheads.

Seeing his foot soldiers go down hadn't done anything to inhibit the sixth intruder. He was the ringleader of this little party, and the stench of hot blood spilled on the floor only seemed to fuel his resolve. His unearthly screech pierced my ears as he rushed me. The beast was lightning fast and lithely agile. I couldn't get a bead on him quick enough to get off a decent shot until he was standing in front of me, so I only grazed his shoulder. I struggled backward, attempting to put enough space between us for a second try, but he wrapped a meaty hand around the barrel and tried to twist the gun out of my hand. My finger still on the trigger, I wanted him to know I wasn't going down without a fight and squeezed my finger. The bullet tore through the fiend's palm, the pungent smell of cauterized flesh instantaneous. The beast's blood ran black and its face contorted, losing its human façade. Feathered fin-like protuberances sprouted from the sides of the creature's wide jaws, and I found myself staring helplessly into the face of a malevolent host of the unforgiving undead, a Sluag.

Before I could react, the Sluag wrapped his ruined hand around my neck and lifted me effortlessly off the ground. Foul-smelling drool oozed from the corners of the creature's mouth. With all the strength I had left, I kicked at him with my dangling feet, but my effort was moot. The brute gave a cruel chuckle and slammed the back of my head into the stout support beam running up the wall. Had I been human, that single blow would have ended me. As it was, the room took off like a carnival

Tilt-a-Whirl, and I had the very human reaction of wanting to throw up. Knowing he had me where he wanted me, the Sluag released my throat, letting me crumple to a limp heap on the floor.

My mind said fight, but my limbs wouldn't obey. I felt myself circling the drain. Just before oblivion took me, a blur of black fur and snarling teeth rushed through the backdoor. In one leap, Roane took the Sluag in the chest, driving him to the floor. With my last tendril of consciousness, I watched Roane's beast rip out the intruder's throat with pleasurable bloodlust.

Then, everything went blissfully black.

Sometime later, I felt the weight of consciousness begin to push around me once again, the throbbing pain in the back of my head guiding me back like a beacon. Unfortunately, being cut off from my family and homeland for so long had weakened me. I'm no longer exempt from pain; nor do I heal instantaneously like I once did, as was my birthright. My own fragility was the worst curse of all.

From the scent of leather and aged wood, I knew I was on the couch upstairs in Roane's office. Even though the lights had been dimmed, any attempt to crack open an eyelid resulted in a critical shot of pain that split through my temples and caused me to silently curse any god who would listen for keeping me in the human world.

"Isa?"

"Unless you're God, go away," I groaned.

"Isa" Roane gently coaxed, "can you move?"

"No."

"Can you at least try?" Roane persisted.

"What part of 'no' don't you under—" I immediately regretted throwing my eyes open and raising my voice. Pain and bile rose up, and I tasted both on the back of my tongue.

Roane placed a quick hand on my forehead. Relief was instant, so I allowed him to hold it there for longer than I wanted to. Hailing from an immortal bloodline much older than my own, Roane's innate healing abilities were strong enough to pass from him to me, something I couldn't even do for myself anymore. When he pulled his hand away, I was looking straight into the amber eyes of his Lupine Glashtyn heritage. A tousle of brown hair flowed to his shoulders, and a long day's growth stubbled his square chin. I sensed his beast just below the surface, ready to emerge at any moment.

"Thank you," my gratitude was genuine, but I despised that it was Roane who could mend me like this.

"Tell me what happened."

Cautiously, I sat up and mentally collected the details before retelling the event. "The first five were amateurs, but that last bastard was a professional. If you hadn't come in when you did and relieved him of that part between his chin and chest... " I shuddered. When I shifted my gaze once again to Roane's eyes, they'd returned to their "human" brown.

"Did any of them say what they were after?"

"No they didn't, Roane, and I was too busy trying to stay alive to ask." I struggled to get to my feet, pettily refusing Roane's proffered helping hand. "Back off and give me a second."

Doing as asked, Roane took an awkward step back then began to pace and think out loud. "Two guys jumped us out back in the alley and shot the suppliers. Gus killed both of them. Now I've got the shipment, Santorini's cash, a bar full of dead guys, and a dead Sluag missionary, but let's handle one emergency at a time."

"Eight?" my voice was much shriller than it needed to be. "Someone sent an eight-man hit squad? Who sends that kind of muscle?"

Roane continued pacing. "That's what doesn't make sense. It couldn't have been The Jesuit; he's the one who turned me on to Santorini since he's retiring at the next moon. If they wanted the shipment, they would have attacked Santorini's men before they got here. If it was the money, the attack would've happened after they left. I'm going to need some time to figure this all out, but first we need to get out of here. We wiped out someone's entire hit squad, and when their boys don't come home, they're bound to come looking."

"Where's Gus?" I asked, suddenly noting the behemoth's protective absence.

"Disposing of the bodies."

"How?" I asked ignorantly.

Roane furrowed his brows, "Do you really want to know?"

He had a point.

"Just so I'm in the loop Roane, what other dealings do you have your paws in that I should know about?"

"Nothing to warrant this kind of attack." Roane hadn't made any sort of denial in regard to other extracurricular activities, which I found a little unsettling.

"Jesus Roane! I don't know if it's good or bad that I'm not the only person you have the ability to royally piss off."

Gus lumbered into the room, his face set in its usual stern calm. "All clear Boss; the shipment's on ice, and the place is locked down." He turned his attention to me, "That was some fancy shooting Isa, but a nasty knock you took to the melon. How you feeling? "

"Peachy Gus, thanks for asking." I tried unsuccessfully not to let sarcasm taint my response.

Roane spoke up, "We need to get out of here. We've stayed too long as it is."

Gus had brought Roane's truck around and parked it at the curb just outside the front door. I got in through the passenger's side and locked the door for good measure. Roane slid in behind the wheel and did the same.

"Take me home," I instructed.

"Home is the first place they're going to come looking for you, Isa."

"So where to then?" I scoffed.

"I have a safe house."

"A safe house?" my brows shot up. "You never told me about any safe house."

"If I'd told you, it wouldn't be much of a safe house now would it?"

Gus knocked on my window and made me jump. I rolled the tinted glass down so he could pass a duffle bag through, which I knew contained weapons.

"Everything you requested is inside Boss, plus some extra ammo and the silver." Gus handed me the same Glock I'd used earlier. "Here you go Isa, since you've already got this one warmed up... "

"Yeah, thanks." I took the weapon and slipped the clip. Gus had taken the time to reload, chamber a bullet, and set the safety. Daemons could be so thoughtful.

"Thanks Gus," Roane replied, "will you be up shortly?"

"In a bit; I have a few feelers to put out on the streets first to see if anyone wants to talk and live to see another sunset."

"Good. See you later."

Gus gave us a short, militant-style salute as we pulled away from the curb. We drove through the sleeping city in silence as I wondered what the hell Roane had gotten me involved with. That's when I was struck by the sobering realization that I should probably feel remorse, guilt—something, anything—because I'd just killed six of my own kind. Fae penalty for killing Fae is a true death. No banishing. No jail. No passing go.

Little did I know what lurked in the dark was worse than banishment. Or death.

Contributors

Larry Anderson is a retired college professor living in Molalla, Oregon. He enjoys the luxury of living close to his children, grandchildren, and great-grandson. A lover of poetry, he is a member of The Molalla Writers Group, Silverton Poetry Association, and Friends of William Stafford. Larry is very active in public poetry events such as open mics and tributes to famous poets. The poem "Owl" was originally published in Larry's first chapbook *Off Camera* in 2011.

Lynn Blatter is a retired florist designing for Teleflora, belonged to AIFD (American Institute of Floral Designers), and has lived in all four corners of the United States. She moved to Oregon in 1999, resides in Mulino with her husband Rocky, is director of the local nonprofit Molalla Communities That Care, and trained for the Molalla Community Emergency Response Team. She is working on a historical novel set in Molalla and Portland, and can be reached through Facebook or at lessabt@molalla.net.

Glen L. Bledsoe is so involved with his hobbies that he hardly has time for his day job. That's not true. His day job as an art/tech teacher and his hobbies have fused together to the extent that it's no longer possible to tell which is which. Glen is also a consulting hypnotist. If you want to find out how he got into that occupation, ask him sometime. He and his wife, Karen, live in Salem with many cats. glenbledsoe@mac.com.

Rebbekah Brainard is a recent college graduate of Political Science and Economics who now seeks to figure out life and travel as much as humanly possible. She writes with the aim to inspire, educate, and entertain, and is currently working to make a career out of writing. She loves all things dragons, goats, and adventure, and runs a farm in Oregon City. She also blogs at awakedragon.wordpress.com and can be contacted through there.

Jacqueline Carl is the co-director of the American Wildlife Foundation (www.awildfound.org), an Oregon nonprofit wildlife care clinic and center for conservation education. She is the author of two books (www.

jajacquest.com), *Whispers from the Wild: Stories from a Wildlife Center* (nonfiction, 2013), and *Seasons of the Wild, a Wildlife Center Mystery* (fiction, 2015).

Rick Carl is a retired fire fighter/medic, law enforcement officer, and state humane officer. He has a background in music, so the rhythm of poetry just comes naturally. His poetry is an expression of a lifetime of work in these professions, and his experience working with animals.

Dani Clifton is a return contributor to *Analekta*, and has previously been published in the *Clackamas Literary Review*. Her noir-fantasy fiction can also be found on Smashwords (as DJ Clifton). When she's not writing, Dani is an intuitive medium and healer at Soulutions NW (www.soulutionsnw.com).

Erin Devlin grew up moving between Oregon and Asia. She attended Georgetown University in Washington, DC for a BS of Foreign Service, and an MA of Latin American Studies. Sharing her fictional writing with others is new for her, so she was nervous to submit to *Analekta*. She enjoys spending time in the outdoors and playing ultimate frisbee. You can contact her at erin.teresa.devlin@gmail.com.

John Flavin was born in Detroit, Michigan. At twenty, he moved to Seattle where he earned two degrees from the University of Washington and later a master's in education. He writes in all genres, including the completed manuscript, *The Big World,* which is a satirical novel about the one, real Afterworld. Mr. Flavin is now a high school English teacher and has been writing articles for *The Oregonian* and other publications for over nine years.

Susan Sweetland Garay was born and raised in Portland, Oregon. She lives among the lovely vineyards of the Willamette Valley with her husband and daughter. She enjoys writing, photography, and making art. Her poetry and photographs have been published in a variety of journals. Her first full-length poetry collection, *Approximate Tuesday*, was published in 2013, and was nominated for a Pushcart Prize in 2014. She is a founding editor of The Blue Hour Literary Magazine and Press. Her work can be found at susansweetlandgaray.wordpress.com.

Kate Gray. Kate Gray's first novel, *Carry the Sky* (Forest Avenue Press, 2014), attempts to stare at bullying without blinking. She is the author of three poetry collections, and has also published essays. She and her partner live in a purple house in Portland, Oregon with their sidekicks, Rafi and Wasco, two very patient dogs.

Nichelle Halseth has been writing poetry since she was four years old. Encouraged by her mother, also a poet, Nichelle has continued to grow with each journal filled and each lesson learned. This is her first published poetry. If you would like to reach Nichelle, please feel free to email her at nichenw@gmail.com.

Angie Hughes lives in Vancouver, Washington with her husband, son, and rambunctious Scottie dog, Mr. Chips. She and her family recently spent a completely untethered year on the road, exploring Oahu, England, Ireland, Northern Ireland, Wales, and Scotland. Her newfound favorite things are snorkeling, Airbnb, and sleeping in one bed for more than three nights. She holds an MA in Theatre from the University of Maine. (amhcreations@hotmail.com).

Heather L. Nelson lives with her family on a farm in the foothills of majestic Mount Hood in Oregon. She takes care of two grandchildren while their parents are working, and she recently rescued several starving horses. Heather began writing children's stories for her grandchildren, and has four published books: *Daisy the Protector Dog* (for young children); *First Summer with Horses* (for teens/preteens); *Minerva's Maneuvers* (for ages 8-12); *Lost Family: FOUND!* (for adults), written with her unknown brother, Anthony D. Leonard.

Sandra Rokoff-Lizut feels honored to have received an Oregon Poetry Association's Award. She is a retired educator and children's book author, member of OPA, and Mary's Peak Poets and Poetic License. Sandra has studied poetry at Oregon State University, attended workshops at Centrum, and taught poetry at the Corvallis Boys and Girls Club. Publications include: *The Bicycle Review*, *Wilderness House Review*, and *Wild Goose Poetry Review*. Sandra lives with her husband and three cats in Oregon.

Kelly Samarah lives in Salem, Oregon with her two children and two spoiled dogs. When she isn't busy on her latest writing venture, she passes her time with reading, cooking, and of course, painting. You can learn more about her, and her current projects, by visiting her on Facebook, www.facebook.com/kellysamarah.

Devon Seale is a returning contributor to *Analekta*. He has been developing his fantasy world since high school, if not before. *Analekta* is, to him, an important step in developing his writing and sharing his stories with the world. If you are interested in learning more about his work, he's available at dseale356@gmail.com.

John Sibley Williams is the author of eight collections, most recently *Controlled Hallucinations* (FutureCycle Press, 2013). Four-time Pushcart nominee, he is the winner of the HEART Poetry Award and has been a finalist for the Rumi, Best of the Net, and The Pinch Poetry Prizes. John serves as editor of *The Inflectionist Review* and Board Member of the Friends of William Stafford. Previous publishing credits include *American Literary Review*, *Nimrod International Journal*, *Rio Grande Review*, *Inkwell*, *Cream City Review*, *RHINO*, and various anthologies. He lives in Portland, Oregon. www.johnsibleywilliams.wordpress.com.

Esther Wood, when not writing, enjoys her grandchildren, gardens, and walking her two dogs at least three times every day. After years of subbing, she retired and now tutors two students. She is relatively active on Facebook as an administrator in several groups. She also attends several meetings every week. Zume's story, *Useful Equipment,* started out as a short story, but has grown into a novella. It will be published sometime in 2016, authored under the pen name of E. J. Starwood.

***

Olivia Croom is a graphic designer living in New York City. Visit her website at bit.ly/oliviacroom.

Jennifer Funrue is a crime fighter by night (911 dispatcher), and wife, mommy, and photographer by day. She has three children, a dog, and two frogs. She has worked for newspapers as a photojournalist, freelanced for magazines, and has published work in other media outlets. She is rarely seen without some sort of camera in her hands. She works out of the Salem area, but travels for portrait sessions. One of her earliest memories is holding a camera and capturing everything around her.

L. Lee Shaw is the owner of the independent publishing house, Boho Books. Through Boho, she has published two novels, *Blood Will Tell...* and *Monster Child*. She has also facilitated the publication of nine other novels, a poetry chapbook, short stories and a prior anthology, *Mo' Allie*. Shaw has also taught fiction writing, formed a long-running writer's group, hosted a regional writer's conference, and had two plays produced and performed. For more information, go to www.bohobooks.com.

Heather Frazier works as a freelance editor, helping authors of all genres to polish and perfect their written works. She received both her BA in Arts & Letters and her MA in Book Publishing and Writing from Portland State University in Portland, Oregon. She lives in a soon-to-be empty nest in Molalla, Oregon with her amazing husband and their many pets. For more information, contact her via email at editorfrazier@molalla.net, or look her up at www.bohobooks.com.

Our Thanks

From the hip streets of urban jungles to quiet enclaves tucked in the shadows of Douglas firs, Oregon is known for its rich diversity of people, cultures, and topography. Equally diverse and rich is the talent that lies between mountain and ocean. We have again gathered within the pages of this, our fourth volume of *Analekta*, a rich harvest of fiction, nonfiction, and poetry.

    Bouquets of thanks go to my co-editor, Heather Frazier, whose skillful and careful eye brings each piece to the fullness of its potential. And it's a high-five to our book designer, Olivia Croom, who takes it all in hand and styles it into a thing of beauty. Thank you for always making us look so good!

    But the biggest kudos must go to our contributors, for without them, we would not exist. To each and every one of you… thank you for being so amazing!

~L. Lee Shaw

What an honor to have been a part of this beautiful labor of love we call *Analekta* for the fourth time around. Many thanks to L. Lee Shaw for all her hard work in getting this book out into the world once again. I will forever worship Olivia Croom's dazzling design talents; all hail the Goddess! And to our wonderful contributors, thank you for making this volume possible.

~Heather Frazier

Analekta **Submission Guidelines**

Submission period opens yearly January 1st, and closes June 30th.

Contributors need to reside within the state of Oregon to be eligible for publication in this anthology.
    We welcome all forms of writing for consideration: Fiction; creative nonfiction; poetry; genre fiction novel excerpts, et cetera.

We **do not** publish genre works of:
Children's stories
Children's poetry
Young Adult
Religious
Erotica
Dark fantasy

We accept both hardcopy and digital submissions for consideration. Submissions should be formatted in a Microsoft Word document with 1" margins; the document should be set in a 12-point Times New Roman, Cambria, or Ariel font; the document should have numbered pages. The author's name, physical address, email address, phone number, genre and/or form of writing being submitted, and the title of the work(s) should be included on page one of the submission. For example:

[Contributor Name Here]
1127 Whatever DR
Somewhere, OR 97000
contributorsemail@gmail.com
503-555-5555
Fantasy Fiction piece
Fairyland Adventure

Hardcopy submissions should include an SASE and be sent to: Boho Books 36179 S Sawtell RD, Molalla, OR 97038.

Digital submissions should be emailed to: analekta.molalla@gmail.com.

Minimum acceptable story length is 500 words; maximum length is 3,500 words.

We do accept works that have been submitted to other publications simultaneously, but ask that authors inform us upon submission if this is the case. We also ask for authors to notify us if their work has been accepted for publication elsewhere so that we may withdraw that submission from our selection process.

Upon acceptance for publication in *Analekta*, authors retain all rights to their works published therein.

Please send only one short story, up to four poems, or one creative nonfiction essay per submission.

Authors included in *Analekta* will receive one free contributor's copy upon publication.

For more information about *Analekta,* please visit the Boho Books website at www.bohobooks.com, email L. Lee Shaw or Heather Frazier at analekta.molalla@gmail.com, or find us on Facebook at http://www.facebook.com/analekta.anthology.

CPSIA information can be obtained
at www.ICGtesting.com
Printed in the USA
FSOW01n1747121215
14107FS